BECOMING ALL LIGHT

The Non-Dual Heart of Christianity

Jory Pryor

Printed in the United States of America.

For more information, or to book an event, contact :
jory@methodsofcontemplation.com
http://www.methodsofcontemplation.com

Book design by Jory Pryor
Cover design by Jory Pryor

ISBN - Paperback: 979-8-218-36997-2

First Edition: May 2024

Praise for
Becoming All Light

"As an astute spiritual guide and wise theologian, Jory Pryor, in his book *Becoming All Light*, illuminates profound insights, crafting a tapestry of beauty that ignites the mystic within. Through an exploration of the intersections between Christian theology and diverse wisdom traditions, such as Advaita Vedanta, he invites readers to marvel at the illuminated expanse of the Divine within us all. In this captivating mandala of wisdom, Pryor leads seekers to uncover the radiant essence of their being, transcending boundaries to embrace the limitless Light within."

Mark Karris, *Divine Echoes: Reconciling Prayer with the Uncontrolling Love of God*

"This book is both enlightening and salvific, which becomes understandable once one realizes that Jory Pryor is interested in Advaita Vedanta and Christianity. In reading it, I found nuggets of wisdom and practical insights. The accessible prose made this adventure in nondualism especially enjoyable!"

Thomas Jay Oord, Author of *Open and Relational Theology* and many other books

"There is so much wisdom to glean from this book, it's hard to know where to start. Jory Pryor guides us on a path of transformation towards union with God. This book is rich in wisdom and insight for any traveler of "The Way". Becoming All Light is a true unlocking of the heart of Christianity, which the world desperately needs yet again. "

Heather Hamilton, Bestselling Author of *Returning to Eden*

"So clear, so sweet and refreshing, like cold well water from a tin cup on the hottest day. Just beautiful and utterly clear and direct and essential."

Scott Odom, *The Awakened Heart: Opening to the Unknown on the Path to Awakening*

"An exquisitely wrought book of inter-religious insight and lived experience that exemplifies how sacred texts of one spiritual tradition can shine light on the sacred texts of another, and in ways that enable followers of each tradition to more fully engage with their spiritual path. Through his masterful weaving together of Christian scripture with wisdom from the Upanishads and from particular ancient Buddhist teachings, Jory illuminates and brings sudden and welcome clarity to many of Christianity's more challenging teachings. Jory's profound insights help create an at once remarkable and practical re-envisioning of traditional "Western" understandings of the Christian path, of Jesus' clarion call of metanoia, and how our own lived spiritual journey can reveal our abiding oneness with the Divine. The many times I wrote "yes" and "wow" and "this!" in the margins of this book are too numerous to count. In this time of great change and upheaval in our world, with many of us deconstructing and re-orienting our religious and spiritual vision, what a gift it is to be able to learn from and practice with a living master of inter-religious wisdom. Followers of the wisdom tradition have been waiting for this treasure of a book — a must-read, and one that you will turn to again and again with delight, with awe, and with immense gratitude to its author for the gift of his life-changing insight."

Caroline Oakes, *Practice the Pause: Jesus' Contemplative Practice, New Brain Science, and What It Means to Be Fully Human*

"Philosophy begins with wonder, and mystical theology begins with contemplation. Jory Pryor weaves both of these together in this luminous and insightful exploration of sapiential Christianity in conversation with the world's great nondual wisdom traditions. This book works equally well as a deep dive into western mysticism, and as a roadmap to the many ways that the eastern and western spiritual imaginations guide us into the same heart of compassion."

Carl McColman, author of *Eternal Heart* and *The New Big Book of Christian Mysticism*

2

For my Father, my Enoch, and for Michelle, my Hemalekha.

Contents

"And in this Light one becomes seeing; and this Divine Light is given to the simple sight of the spirit, where the spirit receives the brightness which is God Herself, above all gifts and every creaturely activity, in the idle emptiness in which the spirit has lost itself through fruitive love, and where it receives without means the brightness of God, and is changed without interruption into that brightness which it receives. Behold, this mysterious brightness, in which one sees everything that one can desire according to the emptiness of the spirit: this brightness is so great that the loving contemplative, in their ground wherein they rest, sees and feels nothing but an incomprehensible Light; and through that Simple Nudity which enfolds all things, they find themself, and feel themself, to be that same Light by which they see, and nothing else. And this is the first condition by which one becomes seeing in the Divine Light. Blessed are the eyes which are thus seeing, for they possess eternal life."

St. John of Ruysbroeck: Adornment of the Spiritual Marriage

P r e f a c e

I was born and raised on the fields and farms of the Eastern Shore of Maryland. A child of two young and separated parents, to say we didn't have much would be an understatement. For a good portion of my childhood, I lived in a 600 square foot bungalow out in the country. Our car didn't have heat, so on the ride to school I would wrap up in a blanket on the back seat. The house didn't have air-conditioning either, so in the summer we would lay on the cheap kitchen linoleum and sponge ourselves off to avoid heat stroke. I survived on a robust diet of potted meat and saltines, top ramen, and if we were lucky, some venison from the public forest a few miles away.

I grew up hunting and fishing with the men in my family and harvesting snap peas with the matriarchs. Faith was a big component of our family, and every Sunday we would go a mile or two to the rural Methodist church on the hill, sing the beautiful old hymns from the dusty hymnal, and head downstairs to have toast and coffee with the patriarchs. My grandfather on my father's side occasionally would teach on scripture, and my grandmother on my mother's side had left the family to pursue ordained ministry. But I remember the first time I really noticed something for me in all the accouterments of what I thought was church. I was at a summer Baptist camp, one of the only faith-based summer camps in the area at the time, and it was typically filled with kids doing various farm-themed activities out in the sunshine. But once a week, we got to go into the nearby sanctuary and sit with these little copies of the New Testament. The words of Jesus were boldly written in red, jumping off the page at me. I couldn't fully understand or articulate what it was that drew me to them, but I knew they were important, and I wanted to know more.

I craved this dimension of depth that Jesus' words alluded to - the kingdom of heaven, the pearl of great price, the mysterious spirit animating all hearts. I could occasionally get a taste of that depth-dimension when deep in worship, but as soon as the sermon began, it was nowhere to be found. I wanted something real, tangible, unchanging. Something that wouldn't begin and end with a particular set of chords or an emotional posture. But because of the exclusivist mindset of the Christianity of my culture, any outside sources were strictly off limits. I began reading the gateway drug of Harry Potter, and became interested in sacred ritual, often hiding books and spiritual paraphernalia in a false drawer in my dresser. Through martial arts and Takuan Soho's The Unfettered

10

Mind, I became aware of Zen Buddhism, and immediately took to disappearing into the forest behind our small rancher to practice silent meditation for hours. It struck me as not too dissimilar from what I would do whenever me and my Dad would go hunting. We would of course be looking for food, but while we awaited the gift, I would simply allow my mind to dissolve into the mottled canopy of the loblolly pines. After about an hour or so, everything would be completely radiant. Luminescent, but not with a merely visible light. It was more like a shining through of something from within. I knew that this had to have some connection with those wine-colored words that soaked into me as a child.

I couldn't openly search for explanations outside the Church, so for many years I glued myself to the binding of books by C.S. Lewis, Charles Spurgeon, and when I was feeling particularly bold - Rob Bell. There was obviously more here, more accessibility than what I was accustomed to. But it still seemed like a temporary stop on my journey. I church-hopped for a few years as a young adult, eventually landing at a small church-plant offshoot of a small church-plant. It was led by a former worship leader, and Ph.D in Hebrew Bible. In his sermons, we would explore ancient near-eastern historical context, literary genre, apocryphal texts and commentaries. He seemed to be able to pull aside a curtain of time to see behind the text and into the minds of those souls that put words to their own experience of the Divine. I began to dive back into the core of Christianity, this time uninhibited by the naive fear of Catholicism and otherness that often plagued the church halls of my upbringing. In the words of the desert fathers and mothers, the Cappadocians, in the early-medieval scholastics, the Trappists, the Carmelites, and others I found the depth that I was seeking. It was there, the whole time right beneath my nose. Because of this newfound depth, I immediately understood that like a great aquifer, it wasn't solely restricted to the bedrock of Christianity, but was intertwined with subterraneous veins and capillaries to the groundwater of the entire spiritual world. I couldn't help but feel that accessing these other waters would give me an even deeper glimpse into the waters that birthed devotion in my heart.

That was when I picked up the Bhagavad Gita, The Song of the Lord. And through its pages, Krishna seemed to call to me, illuminating the words of Jesus in a way that made them real, experiential, tangible. I sought out this wisdom like a drowning man seeks air. Not out of a thirst for conceptual knowledge, but more like a deep longing to know every detail of your Beloved's heart and curve of their form. I played spiritual dilettante for a spell, concluding my courtship with all of God's disguises, and then finally came to rest in the non-dual schools of Vedanta, where I met my teacher, Jim. He wasn't some majestic guru from India, he was just a kind old white man with low vision from California. But he wielded the sword of knowledge like a claymore, and not just told me, but *showed me* what both Jesus, and Krishna were always talking about. He seemed to be able to rummage around in my own heart and pull out the gems that I had long ago locked a way to collect dust. He brushed them off and with great compassion, gave me back what was already mine to begin with. Every word he spoke seemed to feel like an echo of what was already sounding silently in me. And through that mirroring of innate wisdom, I came to see that who he really was, and who I really am are not different in the least. And it is that very same gift that I believe enlivened the mind of Jesus, and those who faithfully followed him. It is that gift that I one day hope to be fortunate enough to in some small respect give away myself.

And here is where an author would typically try to convince you that this book needed to be written. That there was a gaping chasm within the corpus of Christian mystical literature that was waiting patiently to receive the gift of my unique revelation to be rendered complete. At least, that's the typical subtext.

But that isn't what I'm going to tell you. There have been countless other contemporary writers who have boldly and expertly contributed to the global discourse of spiritual thought. Some of them academics, some of them devout spiritual leaders, and some of them dedicated laypersons. Many of these folks I would consider my teachers, and a few of them I'm privileged to call friends. Because of their skillful effort, you will even see some of their writings footnoted in this book. It also goes without saying that any merit contained here is not my own but the legacy of my teachers, and any defects wholly belong to me. I have done my best to stay faithful to classical translations of texts, while updating the language where I felt it was helpful for understanding.

Even though my purpose with this book is born out of the modern age, and inextricable from the cultural and social context in which it came – most of what I'm about to tell you isn't really new at all. It isn't the bleeding edge of inter-religious dialogue, or an intersectional or dialectic synthesis of previously unexamined systems of belief and practice. Nor will I propose that my particular view of the Christian path is the one true view, or even the most proximate interpretation. As so many traditions attest, God is not found in books, and neither is enlightenment.

So, in a way, this book didn't need to be written. There are others who have said similar things with more profundity or a higher degree of clarity, to which I am of course, forever indebted. But in another way, this book needed to be be born specifically because it is the outflow of my own practice. Our embodiment of Source is at its highest fidelity when we too "act as source" by making all we have been given flow again, as Panikkar says. The gift of true teaching is not one to be simply consumed, but is to be *consummated*. And a gift, no matter how precious, is incomplete until it is shared. Whether that be a work of art, a homecooked meal, or wisdom itself.

It is the very act of sharing with the community of people drawn to this content that has stabilized this knowledge in my own experience. And it is the kind words of others that has made me realize the Divine uses every voice in its infinite chorus. That despite the persistent notion that it's all been said before, and that there's nothing of substance I could truly contribute, despite the fact that I am woefully unqualified to be counted among those that have spoken on these matters – nonetheless, God continues to use the ramblings of this jack, joke, poor potsherd to accomplish Her purpose of shining all light through the innumerable facets in the resplendent face of love.

Part One:

Fire

I

I AM THE WAY

ये यथा मां प्रपद्यन्ते तांस्तथैव भजाम्यहम् ।

मम वर्त्मानुवर्त्तन्ते मनुष्याः पार्थ सर्वशः ॥

ye yathā mām prapadyante tāns tathaiva bhajāmyaham

mama vartmānuvartante manushyāh pārtha sarvaśhah

"In whatever way people surrender unto Me, so do I receive them. Everyone follows My path, knowingly or unknowingly, O son of Pritha."
-Bhagavad Gita 4.11

C hristianity is a hard nut to crack. That's the answer I usually give when people ask why I use the teachings of other traditions fluidly with that of Christianity. Much of the writing around the person of Jesus is written in a sort of coded language. This language often uses the genre of narrative story, mythical allegory, theological musing, all weaving together into a beautiful tapestry. But the effect of this tapestry on us often leads to a dewy-eyed and fuzzy-edged type of mysticism in which we feel comforted. But like the warm feeling we might get after time with friends, or after watching a feel-good movie, it doesn't last. It can be powerful, and emotionally moving, but it can lack a clarity that enables the meaning to penetrate into the very way we experience life.

There is such richness and depth within the Christian tradition, but often times we are oblivious to it, or if we are fortunate enough to be aware of its hidden treasure, it feels remote or inaccessible. If you grew up in the western hemisphere, (and likely even if you didn't, thanks to the evangelistic and imperial penchant of the West) you were formed at least in part by the cultural conditioning of the Abrahamic faith. Whether it's in your being named after a biblical character, or being subtly influenced by the messianic themes interwoven with our shared stories and media – the myths and metaphors of Semitic and Greek culture form a sort of substratum to which we all belong.

Because of this ubiquity, we tend to be saddled with a frustrating mix of advantage, and pitfall when it comes to truly engaging with the spiritual path beyond a simple cultural identity marker. One advantage is, that for better or worse, we cannot escape the conditioning we are in – and so the language that is inextricably woven into our sense of identity is the language that is often the most effective in untangling that same tangled knot of the semantic and the subjective.

How we fall is often how we get up.

But because of our proximity (if that can ever be the word) to this structure of meaning, we often miss the forest for the trees. We are *so* close to it that we can no longer see the immediacy and depth of what lay right before our eyes. Which is why, as the archetypal motif of the Hero's Journey attests, we must sometimes leave our familiar setting and attend to something strange yet welcoming, unsettling yet beckoning us onward regardless. And hidden in that invitation is the gift of returning home and being able to see it anew – *even for the first time.*

That is what the teachings of Advaita Vedanta, Śakta Tantra, and Dzogchen Buddhism have done for me. Not because they intrinsically contain a revelation that is not found in the Christian scriptures, but because they have formulated their traditions in a way that render it a powerful and valid *means of knowledge.* Where the dominant spiritual paradigm of our birth tells us densely and historically situated narratives, coded in layers of mythology and theology, other traditions often strip away the husk and give us the nectarine seed of truth unmediated and undressed.

I found this to be the case when I first picked up Eknath Easwaran's accessible translation of the Bhagavad Gita, or *Song of the Lord*. Suddenly, what seemed new and strange was natural and stunningly familiar. Scrawled messily on the margins were scriptural references; passages from the mouth of Krishna that were mirror images of the letters in red from my youth. Words that were once mysterious and inaccessible, through a different context were illuminated and within reach. It is for this reason that, despite having already discovered the contemplative Christian tradition, I often say that it is Krishna that allowed me to finally know Christ in a more intimate way than I could have ever imagined.

Take for example this passage from the Gospel of John:

> Thomas said to him, "Lord, we do not know where you are going. How do we know the way?". Jesus said to him, "I am the way and the truth and the life. No one comes to the Father except through me. If you had known me,

you also would have recognized my Father. From this
moment you know and have seen him."

- John 14: 5-7

This passage is typically a pain-point for post-evangelical, post-
deconstruction Christians that want to see the good in their own
tradition but are unsure how to parse a verse like this that seems
so abrasive and exclusionary. So, what exactly is Jesus saying here?
One aspect to note is that this passage is found in a gospel that is
well known to be the more esoteric of the four found in typical
canon. While it is a bit of an oversimplification, it could be said
that the synoptic gospels of Matthew, Mark, and Luke give us a
glimpse at the life and teachings of the person of Jesus, displaying
in His person the relatable dynamism and growth that we can
relate with as human beings. While the gospel of John in
complement reveals His immutable and eternal nature as the
Christ. In essence, though the words are placed in the mouth of
the person of Jesus, it is not the flesh and bone of the first-century
Jewish rabbi that form the Way to life, but the transcendent
dimension of *being* that he represented. That cosmic metaphysical
principle is what is also spoken of by Krishna in the Bhagavad
Gita, when he says:

"In whatever way people surrender unto Me, so do I receive them. *Everyone* follows My path, knowingly or unknowingly, O son of Pritha."

-Bhagavad Gita 4.11

Though separated by thousands of miles and thousands of years, the divine echo through time and space is unmistakable. But what often strikes our ears as callous exclusivity in the former passage, softens as universal inclusivity in the latter. What if Jesus wasn't claiming unilateral control over the contemplative journey, but instead was hinting that the truth he identified with is the nexus point of all myriad paths? That despite the circuitous way, there is one door that we all come to. The words of the charioteer Krishna to his friend and student in the midst of turmoil highlight the truth that the early desert fathers and mothers knew in the first few centuries of Christianity – that freedom is for everyone. And further: *It is inevitable.*

A MANDALA

"It is time for Christian scribes, or jñanis — to awaken and bring forth from their treasury, as Jesus says, at once things old and things new."

-Nicholas Groves

I am deeply thankful for those from within the tradition that have taken tweezers and a magnifying glass to biblical narrative and offered helpful re-envisioning to assist in the reclaiming of the fruit hidden behind the rind of ancient-near-eastern context. This appreciation isn't just for the Borgs and Brugemanns though. I'm grateful for people like Joshua James, a Ph.D. in Hebrew Bible, pastor, and friend. Each week, Josh studies and synthesizes from weighty tomes and commentaries – pulling out specific and highly relevant details that come Sunday begin to breathe new life into the stories of the Bible. This transmutation enables congregants without the benefit of a seminary education to relate to the characters and their predicaments, seeing them not as intangible historical vignettes, but as living examples of our own story.

I also am reminded of lay-theologians like Heather Hamilton, Caroline Oaks, and Jane Woods, who use the new landscape of social media and virtual community to create a space of engagement with the content of contemplative Christianity. Even without a formal academic background in ancient languages, philosophy, or theology, these powerful women season their reading of the Way of Jesus with the psychological lens of Jungian analysis, or the esoteric dimension of Gurdjieffian work to allow everyday people to drink from the deep and clear waters that lie beneath the murky surface of what normally passes for American religion. I'm especially appreciative of those like my former spiritual director Carol, who are willing to be a spiritual friend, mentoring others and helping to discern what revelation means within the mundane moments of our normal life.

What each of us must ultimately do with the raw material of this tradition that we've inherited is to allow this timeless wisdom to be made manifest in the particularity of our being, in a way that makes us come alive.

> "..In the end, each of us will interpret the Jesus story in the way that's most relevant to us; that is how it should be. In fact, that is how it needs to be, because if we only look at someone else's interpretation, if we only look at it through one lens, then it completely gets in the way of our innate and unique creativity."
>
> -Adyashanti: Resurrecting Jesus

What I aim to do in this regard is not to redo what has already been redone, and if I have it is because of my own ignorance. I have no intention of performing a historical, psychological, theological, or otherwise mythological examination of the Christian revelation. I won't relate the nature of contemplation to neuroscience, nor to quantum physics. As I said in the preface, this work has largely been done, and well, by the countless authors and teachers across the globe. Nor do I intend to simply lay out a series of loose parallels between the Christian and Vedic tradition, without any coherent framework. Rather, my purpose in this is to use the *pramana* of Advaita Vedanta to highlight specific constellations of wisdom within the Christian vista, and carve out of the regolioth a mandala with which to experience and marvel at the illuminated expanse that we call enlightenment, nirvana, moksha, kaivalya, or in our native tongue: *salvation.*

And not just to marvel at it, but to *shine* as that self-same light.

II

HERMENEUTIC AND REVELATION

अद्वैतं परमार्थो हि द्वैतं तद्भेद उच्यते ।

तेषाम् उभयथा द्वैतं तेनायं न विरुद्ध्यते ॥ १८ ॥

Advaitam paramārtho hi dvaitam tadbheda ucyate |

teṣām ubhayathā dvaitam tenāyam na viruddhyate | |

"As non-duality is the ultimate Reality, therefore duality is said to be its effect. The dualists perceive duality either way. Therefore, the non-dual position does not conflict with the dualist's position."
Mandukya Karika 3.18

L ike most faith traditions, Christianity is not a monolith. Despite the frequent refrain of orthodoxy, there is no singular way to interpret scripture. While some may lament the countless denominations and subsets of the Church, it is testament to the vibrant and dynamic nature of truth that can express itself however it needs to be heard by a particular people, and in a particular time. It is that particularity that enables us to access revelation from within our cultural and societal conditioning. So, before we explore the non-dual heart of Christianity, it would be beneficial for us to explore the different hermeneutics that serve the unitive revelation of Spirit.

DUALISM

There are three primary interpretive schools within the Vedantic tradition, all developed as separate hermeneutics on the Upanishads, the knowledge portion of the oldest extant religious text known as the Vedas. One such school is called Dvaita, which simply means "two" in Sanskrit. Its foremost commentator is the sage Madhvācārya (CE 1238–1317), who was a staunch critic of the other two primary schools of Vedanta. Much of the thought of Madhva is resonant with the broad strokes of more conservative Christian theology, that God and the human soul are distinct and discrete entities, never overlapping nor identical. In this system of philosophy, not only is the Divine qualitatively different than the soul, but it is different than nature as well. In fact, there are five fundamental differences or dualities outlined by followers of the Dvaita system.

1. Between various types of matter.
2. Between matter and individual souls.
3. Between individual souls.
4. Between inanimate or insentient matter and the Divine.
5. Between the soul (or jīvātma) and the Divine (or paramatma).

These dividing lines seem to stand out on the page, and we might even be inclined to write some of them off as fundamentally dualistic. But *isn't this the way we see normally in our day to day lives?*

Don't we think that mud and gold are different?
Don't we think that the chair we're sitting on, and our mind are different?
Don't we think that our own self and other people are different?
Don't we think that the county landfill and God are different?
Don't we think that we are different than God?

In many ways, this is often the default mode of our perception. Even if we claim to be modern-day mystics that have received a gift of spiritual experience, our predominant model of perception is usually not far off from someone that hasn't. And we don't have to go far to find extreme corollaries of this line of thinking in our own tradition.

"Let it stand, therefore, as an indubitable truth, which no engines can shake, that the mind of man is so entirely alienated from the righteousness of God that he cannot conceive, desire, or design anything but what is wicked, distorted, foul, impure, and iniquitous; that his heart is so thoroughly envenomed by sin that it can breathe out nothing but corruption and rottenness; that if some men occasionally make a show of goodness, their mind is ever interwoven with hypocrisy and deceit, their soul inwardly bound with the fetters of wickedness."

- John Calvin

Of course, it need not be so stark a contrast to fall into the camp of dualism. It only requires a basic and often subconscious belief that the human being, and God, are substantively different ontological realities. As David Bentley Hart notes, the resurgence from the crypt of a form of dualism called 'two-tier Thomism' has been increasing in popularity within Catholic theological circles. Although examining the deficiencies of this form of thought is beyond our scope here, it is enough to say that it feigns both reason, and the mystical, and so appears seductively similar to those without theological familiarity. And despite the use of florid verbiage by its adherents to drive a wedge between the human and

Spirit, its poverty is apparent to anyone that has had more than a fleeting glimpse of the divine indwelling.

QUALIFIED NON-DUALISM

Another school of the major six within Indic philosophy is that of Vishistadvaita, or qualified non-dualism. This form of interpretation of the Upanishads is known primarily through the commentator and sage Ramanuja (1017 CE – 1137 CE). The main factor that differentiates Madhva's interpretation of the Upanishads, with that of Ramanuja's, is that while the former posits an ontological difference between discrete entities and Divinity, the latter opts for a tripartite expression of Isvara (God), Jiva (person), and jagat (world). This three-fold expression represents a holistic picture of an entire organism, not entirely dissimilar from Martin Luther's expression of the human spirit, soul, and body – modeled after the three chambers of the Hebrew temple. The outer chamber symbolized by the world contains the subtler and sentient form of the individual being, and both of these explicit manifestations are the equally real form of God. A simple analogy that is often used is that of part, and whole – we are the parts, and God is the whole.

This communing of the part with the whole is resonant with much of Christian theology throughout the last two millennia, and especially with the post-deconstruction return to what is often called pan-entheism (or God within all things). God pervades every facet of the world, but God is also infinitely *more* than the world.

> "Christ invests himself organically within all creation, immersing himself in things, in the heart of matter, and thus unifying the world. The universe is physically impregnated to the very core of its matter by the influence of his superhuman nature. Everything is physically "christified," gathered up by the incarnate Word as nourishment that assimilates, transforms, and divinizes."
>
> - Ilia Delio, *The Unbearable Wholeness of Being*

This frame of reference offers a helpful corrective of increased intimacy to nourish our soul from its previous obsession with dualistic separation from the world, from ourselves, and from God. And as such, this healing balm is the goal for many aspirants of theistic religions, including Christianity.

But while this move from viewing God as a distant other to an inclusive embrace is a step in the right direction, there's another way of looking at things that can be even more deeply liberating.

NON-DUALISM

> "Non-duality is the quintessence of Christ's mystery."
> Raimundo Panikkar, *Christophany*

The Advaita (literally 'not-two') school of Vedanta, popularized by the commentator Śankara applies a yet more radical hermeneutic to its interpretation of scripture. In the framework of Advaita, God does not pervade the universe in the same way that smoke pervades the room. In this non-dual revelation, there is *no fundamental difference* between the pervader, and the pervaded. This deeper revelation can be glimpsed from the writings of rare souls from the Christian tradition that risked blasphemy in putting their deepest experience to paper. And some even lost their life for it.

> "Now listen, Reason, says Love, to understand better what you are asking about. A man who is on fire feels no cold, a man who is drowning knows no thirst. Now this Soul, says Love, is so burned in Love's fiery furnace that *she has become very fire*, so that she feels no fire, for in herself *she is fire*, through the power of Love which has changed

35

her into the fire of Love. This fire burns of and through itself, everywhere, incessantly, without consuming any matter or being able to wish to consume it, except only from itself; for whoever feels some perception of God through matter which he sees or hears outside himself, or through some labor which he there performs of himself is not all fire; rather, there is some matter, together, with the fire."

- Marguerite Porete, *The Mirror of Simple Souls*

If you're reading this book, you've likely already been exposed in some way to the Eastern Orthodox conception of *theosis,* the teaching that humanity has the innate potential to become divine not only in participation, but in *nature.* As Saint Athanasius famously said in his *On The Incarnation,* "For the Son of God became man, so that we might become God". This very sentiment is mirrored by the writings of the seers of the Upanishads.

> "They, verily, who knows that Supreme Brahman become themself Brahman; in their lineage none is born who knows not the Brahman. They cross beyond sorrow, they cross beyond sin, they are delivered from the knotted cord of the secret heart and become immortal."
> -Mundaka Upanishad 3.2.9

The fundamental difference then, between pan-entheism, or qualified non-duality and non-duality proper lies largely in their treatment of the phenomenal world. Pan-entheism acknowledges a separate but connected duality between God and the world. God here is both immanent *within* the very world we inhabit, yet also transcendentally *beyond* the world and not exhausted by it in the least. In juxtaposition, non-duality shows not just the theory, but the *praxis* to transcend all dualities – self, other, matter, and even including the stubborn division between the self and the Divine. Non-duality powerfully teaches us that the dualistic perception of separation is an illusion to be *seen through* like a lace curtain over an open window. In this examination, transcendence and immanence collapse into each other so that even the words 'within' and 'beyond' lose their meaning – having no concrete referent.

Here Spirit does not pervade the world like smoke in a room, *but like heat in fire*.

However, these two perspectives need not be seen as mutually exclusive. In fact, there are many areas of convergence and complementarity between Pan-entheism and Non-Duality:

Unity in Diversity: panentheism and non-duality both emphasize the interconnectedness of all existence. Pan-entheism sees this interconnectedness as an expression of the divine within creation, while non-duality sees not only the intricate web of synergistic relations in the web of inter-dependent causality, but additionally the realization of a more fundamental oneness beneath and beyond the illusion of separateness.

The Holy and the mundane: panentheism encourages individuals to see the divine in everyday life, appreciating the sacredness of creations participation in the divine life. Non-duality likewise invites practitioners to recognize the numinous nature of ordinary experience, not by the bringing close or uniting of two disparate realms, but by the unapologetic dissolution of the boundaries that make them separate in the first place. The non-dualist takes seriously Schelling's claim that nature is simply Spirit made visible.

Transcending Ego: Both perspectives advocate transcending the egoic self. Panentheistic spirituality suggests a gradual surrendering to God's immanent presence, sometimes taking a lifetime on the progressive path. While non-dualistic spiritual paths hold space for progressive realization, it also allows in contrast the immediate recognition of the ultimately insubstantial and illusory nature of the ego itself, and thereby allowing Reality to shine in itself as pristine from the very beginning.

The progressive path of religion tells us that the goal is out there somewhere, that it is something to be attained or acquired. The more esoteric paths will say that God is not out there, but baked into the very fabric of reality. But even the esoteric core of most spiritual trajectories says that even though Divinity is intimately intertwined with the universe, it can take a lifetime to have a single glimpse behind the curtain. The direct path, on the other hand reveals to us that not only is God *not* out there in space, but equally not out then in *time* either. The corrective that the direct path of Advaita gives is the emphasis that we are already free, we simply do not recognize it.

What this diversity of hermeneutical approaches allows for is maximum accessibility to Divine truth, regardless of our intellectual, or emotional predisposition. In one way, each interpretive lens is its own method of approach, and in another is its own revelation. However rather than static categories, these three schools of wisdom can be moved through fluidly and dynamically in the life of the aspirant. The non-dual heart is not at odds with dualism or qualification, rather it is their highest consummate *perfection* when taken to its logical end. As no step is too small, the generosity of Gods self-disclosure enfolds all into itself – allowing us graciously to begin exactly where we are and to journey from that humble origin to the source that has no center, nor circumference.

So, with that said, if we are to make a beginning from wherever we happen to be right now, then *where are we?*

III

PURE FROM THE BEGINNING

ātmā sākṣī vibhupūrṇa eko muktaścidakriyah |
asango nihsprhahśānto bhramātsamsāravāniva | |

"Your real nature is as the one perfect, free, and actionless consciousness, the all-pervading witness - unattached to anything, desireless and at peace. It is from illusion that you seem to be involved in samsara."

Ashtavakra Gita 1:12

I would start at the beginning, but I think we need to go farther back. The current trend in both Christian and secular circles is to find one historical figure so culturally anachronistic and morally obtuse that we can blame the entire collapse of civilization or civilized religion on their words. In the minds of many, what Christopher Columbus is to global exploration, or Ronald Reagan is to the confluence of government and economics, Augustine of Hippo is to the Christian religion. Our collective disdain for Reaganomics aside, it isn't uncontroversial to say that these figures and their legacy have impacted the world in a uniquely problematic way. However, to say as many modern theologians do, that Augustine's doctrine of original sin is the smoking gun to the murder of Christ's message, is hyperbole to our own detriment.

ORIGINAL SIN

Although, like scholar and theologian David Bentley Hart, I find myself bored with the unimaginative false dichotomies of God and man, self-effort and Divine Providence, or nature and Grace, that once captured the intellectual imaginations of our predecessors. The ideological battle between Pelagius and Augustine on the topic of whether salvation is solely due to our own self-effort based on innate human capacity, or to the autonomous grace of God's benevolent activity is one that juxtaposes humanity and divinity at odds with each other, and largely misses the point entirely. So rather than fulfilling the ultimate purpose of religion in reconnecting *(re-ligio)* our corporeal and ethereal forms, each camp in taking their own immovable position serves to further divide them from the all-encompassing unity that God represents.

A strict interpretation of the doctrine of original sin has historically acted as the launch pad for colonialist, tyrannical, and racist dynamics of power across the globe (to mention nothing of its repressed sexuality and internalized psychological effect on the essential self-image of its adherents). When taken at face value, the teaching has the net effect of convincing us that we are fundamentally at odds with the Divine in the very nature of our being. The fault, as is proposed by many modern theologians, is easily traced back to Saint Paul, another figure we love to hate. But both Augustine's and our own misreading of the Pauline epistles do us no good in identifying what it is that's being communicated through them. Fortunately, we have collectively shed the old snake skin of any sense of inherited guilt or essential depravity that is often associated with the doctrine. We have resoundingly accepted the theory more consonant with both the Biblical narrative, as well as the early patristics: that of Original Blessing. As described by Matthew Fox at length in his book by the same name, the efficient counterpoint of original blessing redirects our origin story away from a preoccupation with magnifying the beatitude of God at the expense of minimizing the dignity of humanity, and toward a more holistically inclusive sense of our creation in the *Imago Dei*.

As I've hopefully made clear, this beneficial reframing of our relationship with God has the power to turn back the clock on the wasted centuries of our relying on the spiritual fortitude of others for our own justification – empowering us to embrace both a blessed inception, and its terminal corollary in theosis. It is not just that we were made in God's image, but we have the innate capacity to also be transformed unto Her likeness. We are fundamentally *good*, as the text of Genesis attests, and to the fullness of the Good we will be made to resemble.

If this is all the anthropology you need (or can stomach) to be completely at peace and free from suffering, you are to be envied. But for most of us, the mental acceptance of a more charitable doctrine to replace an uncharitable one, while undoubtedly helpful, is not sufficient to free us from our own suffering. That despite the infectious refrain that God has made both humanity and the natural world as good, we still feel a chasm within our self that nothing seems to be able to fill. The endless varieties of pain that we inflict on ourselves and others in an effort to compete for our desires is obvious for anyone that has honestly reflected for more than a moment. And as Father Richard Rohr says often, whatever pain we experience that is left untransformed is bound to be transmitted to others. The anguish inflicted upon us as recipient, instead transforms us into its unwilling vector. Whether it manifests as war and bigotry, control and coercion, anxiety and depression, or countless other ways that each of us suffer the collective and individual weight of existence, it's clear that *something* is wrong. There are precious few souls we encounter in our daily life that seem to genuinely be at peace in a deep and lasting sense. It may all be good, however there's clearly something that appears to be obscuring that good. But what?

A ROSE BY ANY OTHER NAME

All of the great wisdom traditions hold commonalities with each other, both in the exoteric forms of practice and the esoteric consequence of their fruition. Although the formal characterization of the problem, the solution, and the path between them may differ in detail, that same description comes after the shared and unitive revelation that like an ocean of nectar bursts the bounds of all our wineskins. While the pandits of the world quarrel, the mystics speak the same language, and our origin story is no different. So, what do other traditions say about our origin and anthropology? Unsurprisingly, if we look to the paths laid out by other non-Abrahamic cultures, we see that although they may not consider our identity as foundationally flawed, they do each point out the glaringly apparent reality of suffering that we all face.

What the Buddhists call *tanha* or thirst – the active ingredient in the second of the Buddhas four noble truths, the Vedantin describes as *kama, vancha, sprha* – craving, wanting, longing. This existential longing within each of us betrays a deeply seated experience of emptiness or lack, and even though we may not perceive an inherited guilt or hereditary transmission of ontological privation, having evolved past Augustine's Manichean preoccupation, we still feel compelled in our will and seemingly beyond it to shore-up the gaps in our being by reaching out for the fruit of fulfillment from the outside. Thomas Aquinas reframed original sin this way in his magnum opus the Summa Theologica:

"The lust which transmits the original sin to the offspring *is not actual lust*, because given that it were granted by divine power to someone who did not feel any disordered lust in the act of procreation, they would still transmit the original sin to the offspring. But that lust is to be understood *habitually*, according to the fact that the sensitive appetite is not contained under reason by the bond of original justice. And such lust is equal in all." [1]

---

[1] STh Iª–IIae q. 82 a. 4 ad 3.

Aquinas points out that instead of a *libido actualis*, it is rather a *libido habitualis,* or an involuntary tendency to seek fulfilment from the external world. The mind in itself is primarily tasked with avoiding pain, and seeking pleasure – no doubt a helpful occupation in terms of preserving the life of an organism in the grand song of human evolution. As the Katha Upanishad proclaims, God has created us with our senses directed outward as a natural way to operate in the world, and so it is just as natural to see the continuance of that external sensory orientation to arrive through the process of human procreation. In other words, we look for our fulfillment *out there* because that's what our parents did, and their parents, and so forth. Transmission of this impulse for gratification aside, a proper exegesis of Paul's letter to the Romans (Where Augustine found basis for his own misguided conclusions) identifies not a mechanism of the spreading of sin from one to all, but from center to periphery:

> "Therefore, just as sin entered into the cosmos through one man, and death through sin, so also death pervaded all humanity, whereupon all sinned;"
> Romans 5:12

47

The "one man" clearly references Adam. But Adam is not merely the name of a physical man or first patriarch, situated at the beginning of a sacred timeline stretching forth from then to now, but the atemporal *symbol* for our sense of identity: the core of who we believe ourselves to be. So, the chiasmic structure of Adam, sin, death, and death, sin, humanity is not one of genealogical or temporal significance, but one of spiritual and eternal weight. It is not that the man Adam sinned once, and as a result humanity reaps the consequences either *in him* or *because* of him. Hart booms, "..there was no fall 'back then' in historical time, either for the race or for the individual."[1] It is rather that Adam is the signifier for that part within each of us where we each engage in *hamartia*, in missing the mark. Sin doesn't proceed from some alpha-point of time in the distant past toward our present, but seemingly from the depths of our own existence.

Though it may at first seem damning that instead of being able to blame our current karmic predicament on some mythical figure, that we in Marxian fashion actually contain the seeds of our own destruction, it is more properly liberating because that means we *also* contain the innate capacity to destroy them. It is precisely because the problem itself is not *out there,* that the solution isn't either.

THE KNOT OF THE HEART

One of the many oddities of the English language is that the word *ravel* means the same as its opposite – *unravel*. To really pull something apart and examine it, is therefore on one hand a deconstructive act, but on the other hand, a positive one in its revealing of what formerly was an opaque assemblage of tangled components to be nothing more than a relationship of individual strands. The overarching theme of the spiritual path is much the same – one great and continuous unraveling of our mistaken notions and unspooling into the mystery of being that recedes ever before us like an infinite horizon. And the first part of that unraveling (or raveling) is knowing where to begin.

Before we destroy the seed of our misplaced impulse for completion, we need to know where it comes from. While much of Western Christianity focuses on the will and action as the primary modality in which God does Her work, due to the primary conception of theosis being a union of the finite will with the infinite, the wisdom of Advaita incorporates not just volition and action, but also cognition. Before there's a movement of will in the form of desire, there lies its inherent cause: a movement of knowledge in the form of ignorance.

Adi Śankara in his *Upadeśa Sahasri* (Thousand Teachings), speaks of a specific causal sequence of our suffering.[2] This causal cascade begins with primal nescience or *avidya*, resulting in what Aquinas termed 'habitual desire' or *kama*, and producing the movement of action toward our perceived desire or *karma*. This karma in turn produces the dualistic perception *dharma* and *adharma*, or good and evil. This constitutes the *hridaya-granthi* or three-fold knot of the heart that serves as the basis for the entire drama of human suffering. And this knot, when properly untied opens up the non-dual heart of Christianity, whose beatitude is reflected as abiding peace, immovable joy, and the absence of fear.

While typical exegesis of the Genesis myth highlights the disobedience of Adam and Eve's action against God's commandment, contained within the story are the subtle whispers of the causal chain used by Śankara in his exposition of Vedanta.

> But the serpent said to the woman, "You will not die, for God knows that when you eat of it your eyes will be opened, and *you will be like God*, knowing good and evil."
> Genesis 3:4-5 NRSVUE

In this primordial lie of the serpent, we are told two things primarily:

1. We are implicitly told that we are *not* like God as we are presently.
2. That in order for us to acquire God's likeness, we need to attain the object *out there* that has the power to divinize us.

ORIGINAL BLESSING

Taken at face value, this passage spoken by the serpent is no different than the typical claim of original sin: that we are fundamentally flawed, and we must attain to the Divine from a source outside our being. So instead of solving the problem, the doctrine reifies it in terms of an ontological transition between the fruit of the tree of the knowledge of good and evil, and Gods own self. This is of course, all in the third chapter of Genesis. But in the previous creation account in chapter one, we are told something very different:

> "So God created humans in his image, in the image of God he created them."
> Genesis 1:27 NRSVUE

In the first account of creation, we are already told in no uncertain terms that the very nature of our origin is one of Divine similitude; the import being that the fundamental lie told in the second allegory is that we are not *already* Divine by nature of our very being. This fundamental *avidya* leads us to believe that we are defined by lack and as privation itself; the consequence of which is that we will be propelled by *kama* to seek and fulfill that visceral lack not by looking within to our essential nature, but beyond it to the alluring scent of the fruit beyond. We then engage in *karma* to achieve that ever-shifting holy object that will render us whole and complete. It is these three lies that tangle over, under, and through each other to form the dense and matted knot of the heart that constricts our self-knowledge and inherent fulfillment. And we buy it – lock, stock, and barrel.

BLESSING IN DISGUISE

Whether we call it original sin, lust, samsara, bondage, or suffering, it scarcely matters. What all effective wisdom streams do is start from exactly where we are, which for most people is having a deep and largely unexamined belief that they are a separate individual person living in a world that doles out joy and misery from the outside. This joy is to be sought by acting in the world to serve our own interest, and its mirror image of suffering is to be avoided at all costs. So, if you're suffering in any respect – be that as an acute perception of your own finitude, or simply as fear and unhappiness – the origin stories tell us where to begin. And our own story, reframed in light of the causal chain, allows us to go ever backward. Beyond the external actions we perform, beyond even our internal will to acquire our desire and assuage our mistaken sense of lack, to the first link in the chain: ignorance of our true nature. That is perhaps what Augustine meant when he said in his Confessions:

"You have made us for yourself, O Lord, and our heart is restless until it finds its rest in you." [3]

That is the point that Advaita Vedanta repeatedly drives home, and so in this light, original sin becomes not a problem to be solved by behavior modification, not even by renunciation, but a misperception corrected by knowledge. In light of this reframing, our primary missing of the mark is not a problem of our *being*, but of our *knowing*.

Our sin isn't an ontological issue, but an *epistemological* one.

Sin is not original because it is essential to our being, that much is clear. Rather, it is original because, like Adi Śankarācarya says, it is *beginningless*. Like in the middle of a beautiful or terrible dream, we never stop to examine how it is that we found ourselves there. The opening credits do not play for the film of our unknowing. In the same way, could we say the happenings in the movie, or the dream really begin at all? Really, we are always free. But, when the mind has full trust in that freedom and allows it to influence all our apparent activity, that is freedom in this life.

Reframing the doctrine of original sin not as an ontological flaw, but an epistemological smudge on the lens of our knowing - reveals that rather than sweep our unconsciousness under the rug, we can see that the problem is not 'out there' at all. Nor is it 'in here', but instead is the sleep in our eyes that diffracts reality into 'in here' and 'out there' altogether.

IV

THE WELL-WORN PATH

"Now that light which shines above this heaven, higher than all, higher than everything, in the highest world, beyond which there are no other worlds, that is the same light which is within man."

Chandogya Upanishad 3.13.7

A s we begin to unspool, we will inevitably find that we are becoming laced into a new mandala, with nothing wasted. To untangle the dense nest of knotted rope that keeps us bound is the same as to weave a new tapestry, utilizing every frayed end we previously unwound. Likewise, to deconstruct from our tradition of origin is an essential part of faith. It reveals the potentially harmful beliefs we were given. Teachings that may have originally been meant as tools for our liberation, but have been disformed into obstacles to freedom. Bravely taking apart our system of relation to reality and scrutinizing it allows us to step out from under its control. But a lot of practitioners afterward get stuck there in a space of constant uncertainty and loss.

We can't base our life on what we *don't* believe in.

And although perpetual iconoclasm is beautiful, we all reach a point where we ask ourselves not just what's false, but what's *true?*

RAVELING

Although deconstruction in the contemporary scene is a stage that must be moved past, we need to continually stay in the state of unknowing. Ironically, Deconstruction itself can become a new identity, a type of premature reconstruction. That too, must be deconstructed by resolutely refusing to accept any limitation to our path. And although reconstruction proper is a healthy way to reintegrate some of the concepts that were deconstructed, a way of saying, "what do I do with this now?" - care should be taken to not let that new conception become anything other than a conception. As Joseph Campbell often remarked, the menu is not the meal.

So how do we re-orient ourselves to the spiritual path after deconstruction and reconstruction? Two tools that are essential for the contemplative journey post-deconstruction are your intent and your insight:

Your intent, or your *desire* is the inclination of your will directed toward the Divine. The late contemplative theologian and psychiatrist Gerald May called this a "willingness" as opposed to a "willfulness". Or, what Patanjali in the Yoga Sutras calls *Isvara pranidhana:* trustful surrender to the Lord in all things.

We actually *already* have a will directed toward God, but most of the time it is clouded over by a layer of confusion about who we really are, what this world is, and the relationship between the two. This innate orientation toward the Good as we best know the Good is our *dharma,* our nature.

The second supply is our insight, or the trajectory down which we send your will. To what do we direct this innate desire we all possess? It is equally a recommended trajectory for where to rest our desire, and also an admonition against the misplacement of that desire. This insight is best represented not as written instructions, but as a conceptual map of sorts. Fortunately, map or no map, we are all led to the inevitable reality of God, as She turns the terrain Herself when we wander off our path. Really the entire scope of reality is nothing but path, and so we cannot truly become lost. The entire organism of the manifest universe is self-existent, self-revealing, and self-correcting at all levels. There are people throughout history who have undertaken this journey before and haven't had access to, or haven't needed, a map. However, just because someone else was able to overcome all obstacles, doesn't mean we should try and best them. At some point some adventurous soul hiked through the wilderness without a map or guide because there wasn't yet one available, but that doesn't mean that we have to be the explorer and try to do it without one now that they exist.

If someone you knew was traveling into the backcountry of the mountains without a map, you would probably try and convince them it's a smart idea to take one. But so many of us were given a crudely drawn and inaccurate map when we were taught about God. We may have been told that we must earn our way to heaven with good deeds, or that we have to pray a specific prayer in order to not be punished by God for merely existing. These maps and stories can get ingrained into us during childhood, and remain there unconsciously even in adulthood, misleading us on our journey with the Divine. Much of religious upbringing can be based on fear, scarcity, ego building, rule following, and behavior modification. Because of this misinformation, a lot of Christians can be conditioned to be fearful of other faith traditions or spiritual paths, including even their own.

Unfortunately, this narrow interpretation of the spiritual path creates, and continues to lead others into, a constricted sense of faith based on rules, regulations, and fear of the world and of God, instead of the radical trust that is exemplified in the life of Christ. It also prevents us from seeing the richness of theory and practice of a tradition that spans more than 2,000 years. It is for this reason, that occasionally, a new map is necessary that reveals to us the territory in which we travel.

VERNACULAR

A complete whirlwind of misunderstanding can arise when two people who agree talk about something using different terms, and likewise when people who disagree use the same terms. The way we understand concepts begins with words, because in reality words are simply conceptual boxes that we place meaning into. And as that box gets passed from person to person, definitions and connotations are tossed in as well as taken out.

Contemplation itself is not a new concept by any means. In fact, contemplation is a word that stretches back as far as the origins of Christianity itself. Etymology – the history of words and their meanings, is an extremely valuable tool to have in our spiritual toolbelt. It helps us to see how words and their definitions can change over time. This is especially true when a word is translated from one language to another. Often this results in a definition which loses part of its meaning or even turns out to mean the complete opposite of the word's original or intended usage, which is where the phrase "lost in translation" comes from. Contemplation is one of these words, and it has shifted significantly at least four times throughout history.

When most western readers hear the word contemplation, they may typically think of the statue of "the thinker" where a man leans his chin against his hand in deep thought. However, this is not what we mean when we use the word contemplation in the spiritual context.

In the Christian tradition, what we think of as 'thinking' is normally referred to as meditation. This is different than how we westerners typically use the word, having been exposed to the global migration of Buddhist teaching. When we use the word meditate, we often associate it with sitting quietly and "not thinking". The terms now seem to have an antithetical meaning to their original context, which adds a layer of difficulty for inter-religious dialogue.

The word contemplation comes from the Latin *contemplatio* – which when dissected has the components of *con* (with) and *templum* (temple), and originally had the meaning of marking out a space to observe the heavens and receive wisdom. Because each and every language is culturally situated, whenever a word is translated it tends to lose some of its original semantic weight and cultural significance, and that's exactly what we see here. Because the word wasn't just created from Latin.

In fact, *contemplatio* comes from the the Greek word *theoria* which referred to a kind of looking at, or deeply gazing. Historians know that cultures with extended contact tend to absorb and integrate each other's language and customs into their own over time. Sometimes depending on the dynamic of power in the region, this is for less than peaceful reasons, and sometimes it's a survival tactic. It's what happened when the Jews were captive to Babylon, and occupied by Persia, and finally the Greeks and Romans. So, it's no wonder that the early Christians took some of this Neo-

Platonic language and repurposed it for their context. To the ancient Greeks, the process of seeing was a particular kind of knowing. We all have had a similar moment where we seem to be struck with the light of understanding or perceiving something clearly that was previously under a veil of ignorance. That eureka moment when we say, "Oh, I see!". So instead of a *scientia*, or knowing-how – *theoria* was a direct knowing of reality itself.

If theoria was the active verb form of knowing, a Greek noun called *gnosis* was the knowledge that resulted from contemplation. (Yes, as in the gnostics, who are a largely nebulous catch-all, and a misunderstood and diverse subset of early Christians that didn't always agree with the established theology of the empire). Gnosis also shares a linguistic root with the Sanskrit term *jñana* or knowledge, as we'll explore later.

But as early Christianity was steeped in the syncretic, spatial and cultural enmeshment of Jewish and Greek worlds, the Greeks used the word gnosis to refer to a Hebrew word in a book called the Septuagint – which is just a name scholars use to talk about the Greek translation of the Hebrew Scriptures. The Semitic word it was translated from was *da'ath*, which referred also to knowledge, but with the added gloss of intimacy. One engaged not just by the mind, but with love and by the whole person. As in the book of

2nd Samuel, where David entered Bathsheba's tent and he "knew" her.

So, to sum up, we go from contemplation, to *contemplatio*, to *theoria*, to *gnosis*, to *da'ath* – tracing the etymology of the word all the way back to around 1300 BC. The point of all this background is not to amass information, but to show that words and the meanings behind them matter and can change the way we speak and even think about a spiritual teaching, which in turn effects the way we engage with it in our lives. From this simple high-altitude examination, we can see that contemplation has less to do with abstract or conceptual mentation, and even less with extraordinary spiritual experiences, but rather with a direct and unmediated intimacy with reality.

So, what *is* a contemplative?

For the first six centuries, what we now call mystics were referred to in the church as contemplatives. A contemplative is simply a person on the three-fold path of purgation, illumination, and union, slowly and deliberately making their journey toward what Father Richard Rohr calls, "a long, loving, look at the real."

We can see so many examples of this intimate knowing within the pages of holy scripture. In Exodus 3 - It's this vision that Moses saw in the burning bush and on mount Sinai.

It's the gate of heaven in Jacob's vision when he says, "Surely the Lord is in this place, and I didn't even know it."

This piercing truth isn't only found in the Hebrew bible, but through the very namesake of Christianity himself. This relational communion of love and knowledge that we call contemplation is the inward form of prayer Jesus spoke about in the Gospels.

> "But whenever you pray, go into your room and shut the door and pray to your Father who is in secret; and your Father who sees in secret will reward you."
> Matthew 6:6

In following this teaching of Jesus, we leave behind the exterior circumstances and chaos that often fill our environment. We let go of our concerns and worries when we enter our inner room, the deeper interior level of our being. We close that door, not by shutting out the world, but by simply disengaging with our ever-present interior dialogue of judging, comparing, and reacting to people and circumstances.

Over a thousand years later, the Catholic priest and mystic St. John of the Cross wrote, "The Father spoke one word from all eternity and he spoke it in silence, and it is in silence that we hear it." That word is Christ, and the intimate bodily knowing of Christ is contemplation.

So, it's clear that meditation in the true sense, as silent prayer to God where we go beyond our mind in the call to *metanoia*, is a practice that is deeply rooted in the Christian tradition, from the saints through the ages, following back to Jesus, and even to Hebrew scripture. In fact, this is the first teaching Jesus gives after his baptism and the inauguration of his earthly ministry.

> "Change your hearts; for the Kingdom of the heavens has drawn near."
> Matthew 4:17

To be on this interior path is not to go outside the realm of Christianity, but to go *even more deeply* within it. The late father Thomas Keating describes contemplative prayer as "a process of interior transformation, a conversion initiated by God and leading, if we consent, to divine union." This practice results in a complete restructuring of our conscious minds that empowers us to respond instead of react to life's difficulties. It allows us to more acutely and with greater sensitivity perceive the divine presence in, through, beyond, and *as* everything that happens.

When we talk about contemplative prayer, we aren't talking about simply the mental activity of pondering abstract information with our complex minds, but the extremely simple and profound knowledge that's gained only from the intimacy of the heart. If we are to follow the spiritual path outlined by the saints and mystics throughout time, we must upgrade our operating system to one that places our Heart as the core, and the mind as auxiliary. But to do that, we must realize that our mind has already been tied in knots, and our heart has been covered over, and occluded by mistaken ideas about God, the world, and ourselves. The spiritual path in part consists of systematically dismantling these perceptual occlusions that impair our vision of the Divine.

This is what Jesus refers to in the Beatitudes when he says:

"Blessed are the pure in heart, for they will see God."

This purification or purgation of the coverings that obstruct the heart is the first step of a three-fold process outlined by the earliest saints of the Christian tradition, followed by illumination, and finally union.

And that's what we'll explore in the next chapter: how to prepare and purify the Heart as the first step of the contemplative journey. So today, I want to leave you with a short practice to help orient you to the contemplative path.

Make yourself comfortable in whatever space you're in, and we'll begin with a prayer by Catherine of Sienna. As you read each line, either verbally or mentally, close your eyes and repeat each line as a prayer in the depths of your own being. Try to feel the words as she must have felt when she put them to paper, and allow the prayer to be prayed *through* you, leading you surely and gently into deep silence, stillness, and solitude that is always present, just beneath the surface of the mind.

// Meditation //

Pray aloud or silently in the space of the heart:

You, O Eternal Trinity,
You, O Eternal Trinity,
You, O Eternal Trinity,
Are a deep sea into which,
The more I enter,
The more I find.
And the more I find,
The more I seek.
O abyss, o eternal Godhead,
O sea profound,
What more could you give me than yourself?
What more could you give me than yourself?
What more could you give me than yourself?
Amen.

Though at times you may stumble, nothing you do can take you off this path, and you can never truly be lost. For in a sense, this path is all there is. If you slip off the left edge of the trail, you'll stumble back into the right. Even the beginning and the end are two points on an eternal loop. We are all together on this journey into God, and as the late Ram Dass says, we are all simply walking each-other home.

Know that you are safe, held, and loved by God even in moments when you can't seem to see. Now bring your attention to your breath and simply rest in devotion to God. When you're ready, open your eyes and continue your day with this sense of being safe in God beyond your understanding.

V

PREPARING THE HEART

"The lamp of the body is the eye. Thus, if your eye be pure your entire body will be radiant; But if your eye be baleful your entire body will be dark."

Matthew 6:22

There's an old Zen proverb about a learned man coming to the revered Japanese master Nan-in to receive instruction in the way of the Buddha. As is customary, the master served tea to his visitor. He carefully poured the hot tea into the cup placed in front of the guest. The man watched the cup fill until it was overflowing, running over the brim and down the sides, across the table and onto the floor as Nan-in continued to gently pour, seemingly oblivious. The man finally could no longer bite his tongue and shouted, "It is already full! There is no more room!". The master smiled and said, "Yes, like this cup, you are full to the brim of your own opinions and speculations. How can I show you Zen unless you first empty your cup?".

This powerful story doesn't only apply to our mental preconceptions, but also the desires of our heart. The purpose of the initial phase of spirituality is to stoke a *blazing fire* within us. Through the friction against the grain of our habitual patterns, we build a *tapasya*, or heat that begins to burn away all of the dross that clouds the shine of the gold underneath. It is not so much that we must acquire something new, but that we must remove what covers over. As scripture says:

> "But who can endure the day of his coming, and who can stand when he appears? For he is like a refiner's fire and like washers' soap; he will sit as a refiner and purifier of silver, and he will purify the descendants of Levi and refine them like gold and silver, until they present offerings to the Lord in righteousness."
> Malachi 3:2

The degree to which we are emptied of personal egoic desires, is the same degree that we are filled with desire for God alone. The two are utterly polarized opposites, and if our cup is full of selfish desire, it can't be also full of desire for the divine. Personal egoic desires are a way of trying to fill an infinite void that only infinity itself can satisfy. But desire itself is not an impediment to liberation. Every desire that we place as a condition to our happiness is a mediated form of seeking for oneness with God. Every desire is ultimately for the Divine.

Whether it's at the brothel or the bookstore, *God alone is sought.*

There's a reason that mystics of all stripes refer to God as, "Beloved". Because whether we find ourselves in the camp of dualistic devotion, or of uncompromising non-duality, one thing is clear:

God is always the most beloved.

Not only as the source of our fulfilment in the Neoplatonic ascent, but in the bone-deep ache of our longing in the mires of samsāra.

Pouring over sacred texts, or over the curves on the body of a stranger, *the desire is the same.* Every action we take to inch closer to the plenum of *eros*, whether deep into the clutches of ignorance or out into the vast expanse of purified mind - it all reaches its terminus in the Absolute.

Which is *you,* by the way.

Beyond a sense of an economic or immanent Trinity lies the timeless fruition of our craving, our thirsting for living water. And once the reality of that nectar is discerned, *it can never be diluted.*

> "You don't look out there for God, something in the sky, you look in you."
> -Alan Watts

Every time you recognize yourself looking for fulfilment, for happiness, for completeness in something outside yourself - recognize it as a veiled pursuit of the divine. Look inwardly and recognize that it is the divine in you that longs to know itself. Your very desire is evidence of both the existence of its end, as well as its inherent fulfilment.

Most often, we are unable to see clearly this universal desire within our day-to-day fascinations. The blur of our scattered desires seems to cover over our recognition of this truth, and due to this opacity, we only need to peel back the layers of our desire through our action, our will, and our knowledge. So, let's go back to where the practice began, at least in the western world. The term asceticism originally comes from the Greek *askêsis*, referring to intense physical training like that of an athlete. In the early Patristic period of the Church, followers took the word and associated it with practices of self-denial or mortification and preparation for a life of religious devotion. Denial of food, sex, sleep, and possessions was seen as initiation for contact with the Divine and can be found across cultures around the world. The ubiquity of these practices illustrates asceticism's instrumental role as a *means to an end* rather than the goal itself.

The most rigorous programs for ascetics were connected with the monastic desert fathers in the fourth century, continuing on throughout the late medieval friars and beguines, into modern Christianity. The modern spiritual giant Thomas Merton, in New Seeds of Contemplation goes so far as to say, "It can be said that *no contemplative life is possible* without ascetic self-discipline."

Asceticism can sound archaic, baroque, and gaudy: a remnant from times long past. It can even seem inhumane, unhealthy, or barbaric to some modern minds, and often can be. Why would we want to withhold pleasure from ourselves? The first thing to get out of the way is that the process of purgation isn't a rigid moral code of prohibition against alcohol or sexual intimacy (although some of those elements can be present). Purgation is exactly what it sounds like – a purging of toxic elements within ourselves which prevent us from fully seeing and living into the image of God we're made to be. It's a purification of the heart, in preparation for seeing God. This is in reference to the passage mentioned previously where Jesus says:

> "Blessed are the pure in heart, for they shall see God."

Or put simply, Blessed are those whose heart is *not divided*, whose heart is collectively whole, unifying desire and perception.

No double desire, *no double vision*.

Jesus spoke at length of this alchemy of pure desire in his vignettes of the treasure of the field, the dragnet in the ocean, the pearl of great price.

> "Again, the Kingdom of the heavens is like a merchant looking for lovely pearls; And, finding one extremely valuable pearl, he went away and sold all the things he owned and purchased it."
> Matthew 13:45

This pearl is no trinket, but the *cintamani,* the wish-fulfilling gem, or philosopher's stone of the Vishnu Purana. The field in which this treasure is kept is in the green bulb of our spiritual heart. In ancient times, the heart was seen not as a caricaturized hub of fleeting emotions, but as an organ of spiritual perception. That purity of heart is the requisite for divine vision, underscores that this *heart-seeing* was the way for us to come to that intimate *heart-knowing* the tradition describes as contemplation, or gnosis. In other words, contemplation depends on purity of heart, which depends upon purgation. This heart seeing and knowing is the true nature of the illuminative stage of contemplation. But before we can be illuminated, we have to recognize that our perception has been clouded by longing and identification with seemingly external things.

St. John of the Cross says this concerning purgation's place in the contemplative journey:

> "So, they that journey on the road and makes the ascent to God must be habitually careful to quell and mortify the desires; and the greater the speed wherewith a soul does this, the sooner will it reach the end of its journey. Until these be quelled, it cannot reach the end, however much it practices the virtues, since it is unable to attain to

perfection in them; for this perfection consists in voiding and stripping and purifying the soul of every desire."[4]

The process of purgation by means of asceticism in the early church was facilitated by the eradication or transformation of the "passions." This word, like asceticism, has changed over time. This idea of passion comes from the text of the Philokalia, a wealth of wisdom from the early ages of the Eastern Orthodox tradition. As with many ancient spiritual texts, certain words may not directly translate, while others translate but leave behind a deep well of meaning that fades away as contemporary conceptions of that same word arise in the mind of modern readers. Today, the word passion means something akin to an enthusiastic hobby or labor of love we are meant to chase, or perhaps the means by which we chase in our Western "pursuit of happiness". However, this is not the conception ancient readers would have had when reading holy text or practicing their faith. In context, *pathos* in the Greek signified literally that which happens *to* a person or thing, an experience of attachment undergone passively. It is an appetite or impulse such as anger, desire, or jealousy, that violently dominates the soul. Soren Kierkegaard pierces through the noise to say, "For if passion continues in a person, it changes their life into nothing but instants, and as passion cunningly serves its deluded master, it gradually gains the ascendancy until the master serves it like a blind serf."

Many Greek fathers regard the passions as something intrinsically evil, a "disease" of the soul, thus St John Klimakos affirms that God is not the creator of the passions and that they are "unnatural" - alien to man's true self. Other Greek fathers, however, look on the passions as impulses originally placed in humanity by God, and so fundamentally good, although presently distorted by sin. In either view, passions clearly must be eradicated or corrected, and asceticism was a method for doing so.

Another desert father, Saint Isaac the Syrian is quoted referring to the passions as the Christian colloquialism "The World". He says,

> "The world is the general name for all the passions. When we wish to call the passions by a common name, we call them the world. But when we wish to distinguish them by their special names, we call them passions. The passions are the following: love of riches, desire for possessions, bodily pleasure which comes from sexual passion, love of honor which gives rise to envy, lust for power, arrogance and pride of position, the craving to adorn oneself with

luxurious clothes and vain ornaments, the itch for human glory which is a source of rancor and resentment, and physical fear. Where these passions cease to be active, there the world is dead... Someone has said of the Saints that while alive they were dead: for though living in the flesh, they did not live for the flesh (read: ego)."

These passions at their root, come from what is typically described as the false, or small self, in the outer reaches of our interior heart, and manifest in flesh or ego, and distill to form the principalities and power of "the world", which is nothing more than a coalescing and synergy of the individual passions of the soul. So, the method of purifying the intellect, or eye of the heart, by way of ascetic discipline was integral to the conception of sanctification and union with God.

There is not solely a negative disposition in these ancient texts, but the presence of a positive lure for the treasure that lies beneath the tumultuous waters on the surface. In "*On Asceticism and Stillness*", Evagrios the Solitary embraces these views by asking:

> "Do you desire, then, to embrace this life of solitude, and to seek out the blessings of stillness? If so, abandon the cares of the world, and the principalities and powers that

lie beyond them; free yourself from attachment to material things, from domination by passions and desires, so that as a stranger to all this, you may attain true stillness. For only by raising himself above these things can a man achieve the life of stillness."

Evagrios and these bearers of wisdom are saying that within stillness lies the *fullness* of joy, the *radiance* of beauty, and the *peace* of a burden that is light. The obstacle to this interior stillness is attachments, or passions, and the pathway to success is renunciation. Perhaps, the barrier to our enjoyment is not that which stands in the way of our desire, but our desire itself for external objects. Of course, we may think that we have no excessive desire for external things like riches, fame, power and the like, if we could begin to slow and thin the mind, we would see that nearly every microscopic portion of our activity is moved by this desire. From what we say, to whom we say it, to how it is said, to the pre-verbal thought that forms, to the subconscious flow of past impressions – all are moved by desire. It is here that the ascetics advocate for the practice of dispassion, or *apatheia*, a term early Christians borrowed from the Stoic philosophers of the day, signifying a state in which the passions are either uprooted or exercised in accordance with their original purity, and so without committing sin in act or thought. Dispassion then is a state of reintegration and spiritual freedom; when translating the term into Latin, John Cassian rendered it "purity of heart" – alluding to Matthew 5:8. Later still, Kierkegaard identified the purity of heart with the "willing of one thing" and absence of double-mindedness.[5] That is largely what the Christian tradition attempts to do; through loving devotion to God, we surrender both our activity and our intention to be integrated with the intention and activity of God.

This state may imply impartiality and detachment, but *not indifference*. If a dispassionate mind does not suffer on his own account, it is wounded in compassion for its family of all living beings. Counter to some modern understandings, this state at the outset consists, not in ceasing to feel the attacks of desire, but in no longer yielding to them. It is a positive affect, not a negative, similar to the positive peace of Shalom. Evagrios links it closely with the quality of *agape* or unconditional love (unfortunately translated as 'charity'). And Diadochos speaks of the "fire of dispassion" that burns away everything not fundamentally real.

As such, dispassion is among the gifts of God. This is summed up eloquently by Saint John of the Cross in "*The Ascent of Mount Carmel*" when he says:

"For this reason we call detachment the night of the soul, for we are not speaking here of the absence of things – for absence is not detachment, if the desire remains, but of that detachment which consists in giving up desire and losing interest in pleasure. It is *this* that sets the soul free, even though possessions may still be retained. It is not things of this world that occupy or injure the soul, for they do not enter into it; it is rather the wish and desire for them that abide within it."

But as the late Ram Dass says, it's not as simple as just saying "Okay I give all up…Now let me have it". We cannot fool ourselves into the unitive state. This is the domain of the first dark night: the dark night of sense. There's a subtlety and a logical coherence to it, where we can't simply do the right thing for the wrong reason and expect to get the same result. Because to that end, we'd only be cheating ourselves.

THE ACTIVE LIFE

This first *noche oscura* is a purification of the senses where we find that we are not the body, and that we can observe the actions, attachments, and aversions of the body while remaining in that still place of presence that's characterized by the experience of deep *sattvic* peace and equanimity.

This dispassion as Saint Diadochos calls it, is something like the Christian analogue of Buddhist non-attachment. It is the stirrings of the practice of *karma yoga*, renouncing the fruit of our actions in a posture of the fullness of love and devotion. It's where we stop looking to things outside of ourselves to complete us, and allow our desire to be turned inward or toward the fullness of the Divine. This type of spiritual practice is outlined for those that have a firm belief in the reality of the world, and its dependence on God's creation: *srsti-drsti vada,* as outlined in the Vedantic tradition. The world is created outside of us and exists independently, only then are we able to see it.

So how do we perform this yoga of action?

In the Bhagavad Gita, Śri Krishna compassionately lays out a five layered progression of karma yoga: teaching us how to unite our action with the will and knowledge of God. At the most accessible level of practice, Krishna tells us explicitly that our happiness lies not in withdrawing from action in the world, but by taking action. We must initially rouse ourselves from the *tamasic* stupor of inactivity to the movement of *rajasic* dynamism. None of us can last a moment without action of some sort, and so resolving to shake off the heavy blanket of inertia is a universal way of coming into alignment with reality.

Anticipating the question of how exactly it is that we are to act, we are told to act in fulfillment of our *svadharma*, or what is essentially ours to do in the world. This usually implies some admixture of what we are blessed with the aptitude for, and what gives us joy.

Krishna goes on to say that this action should not be simply for action's sake, but should be in a spirit of selfless service to the greater good in the world, however that appears to us.

Where the progression becomes even more difficult is in the admonition to renounce completely the fruit of our actions to the Lord. In other words, when we act in alignment with our abilities to serve society, we do not place the value of our effort solely on what result comes forth from it. We recognize that our action *itself* is valuable insofar as it is an act of dynamic prostration, an act of surrender and worship of the life principle animating all.

And the consummation of this yoga of action is in the direct realization that we are not the agents of action *at all*. It is truly God Herself that is the lifeblood of the universe, making it hum with activity, and teeming with vitality. Jesus himself operated from this sense of karma yoga when he said:

> "I can do *nothing* on my own. As I hear, I judge, and my judgment is just because I seek to do not my own will but the will of him who sent me."
>
> John 5:30

Here, Jesus is revealing the path of renouncing our inherent attachment to the results and outcomes of our striving. He abandons his own will and action not in a sense of apathy or inactivity, but in seeing his own motivation and activity as a ripple in the sea of Gods all-encompassing movement. Later on in John's gospel, he illustrates further:

> "Do you not believe that I am in the Father and the Father is in me? The words that I say to you I do not speak on my own, but *the Father who dwells in me does his works*."
>
> John 14:10

If there was any doubt as to the true doer of action, Jesus dispels it here. Not only does he as an individual not see himself as the agent of action, but he sees all action – *including his own,* as coming from God's own being. Essentially, the broad stream of the Orthodox church takes seriously the claims of Incarnational Theology, in that we are bearers of the *Imago Dei*, but have let that shining image be covered over by our attachments, and once we practice our ascetic *kenosis*, our emptying out of ourselves, that Image can once again shine forth in likeness by the embodiment of the fruits of the Spirit. Once we can imitate Mary and become virginal, in our singleness as *ihidaya*, only then can Christ be born in us.

MATURE VAIRAGYA

Before the contemplative life begins, we are attached to form – the things and stuff of life. We are attached to it because we are literally identified with it. Whether we realize it or not, we send our attention and awareness out beyond ourselves to external things. We become attached to material objects like money, clothing, or the building we live in. We associate ourselves with those temporary things, falsely thinking that our happiness lies within them. If I could only get a bigger house, if I could just get this person to love me, *then* I'll be truly happy.

This process happens on a fluid continuum of attachment and aversion. Picture it kind of like a see-saw, where there's a flat board held up in the middle by a still point. With every circumstance in our life, thoughts and feelings rush out to judge it, resulting either in an attachment to some things, or an aversion to others. We constantly slide back and forth on this continuum all day long in various degrees, which makes it incredibly hard to find our center.

We always feel pulled this way or that way, at the mercy of our passions. Purgation aims to alleviate this first externally by disengaging with the unhealthy manifestations of certain activities that ignite that attachment and aversion cycle – such as food, sleep, and sex. These activities that are so basic to our existence that our attachment to them is at a core level. We find them indistinguishable from ourselves in the early stages, in which we are identified with thinking we are the body. Because if we are just the body, then we have to do whatever the body tells us, whatever feels good, which often is at the expense of our health, or the well-being of others.

This is what Jesus called "Building your house on sand", because all these forms are passing. We first must move away from our identification with ever-changing forms. Our selfish desires are like a great fire. When we realize that giving in to those desires only serves to throw another piece of wood on the flames, we can see that the first thing we have to do is cut off the fuel supply. That flame of desire will keep burning for a while even if we don't feed it – but eventually it will die out. This is what Jesus meant by cleaning of the outside of the cup, then we can move our attention to cleaning the inside of the cup.

Once some distance can be achieved, no specific activity needs to be avoided necessarily, but we can withdraw our attention just a bit more. We are still on the see-saw, just not going all the way to the outsides any longer. Then in anything we do, big or small, we keep watch of our inner faculties while we do it, taking note and observing any attachment or aversion that arises. The closer inside we go, the more centered we become in our being, feeling that still point within us that is silence, stillness, solitude, and spaciousness.

That space is our true home, and is the point at which we find our first illumination. This dark night of sense, as John of the Cross calls it, is where we find that who we are is not the physical body, and that we can observe the actions, attachments, and aversions of the body while remaining in that still place of presence that we've discovered.

Being aware of our attachments and aversions is a way of purifying our desire by becoming empty of desire for the things of the world, and full of desire for God. We can begin to become attuned to the subtle ways our heart moves when we see something we want, we can remain vigilant and recognize that it's just our soul searching for God in the myriad things, and redirect our desire beyond the forms toward God alone.

This is why true and mature *vairagya*, or detachment is really the *vai* (superlative) *ragya* (passion). It is passion and desire taken to its true home, where the thirst of all rivers ends in the ocean of completion. In the end it isn't so much an act of will in opposition to the way things appear to us. Rather, it is the outcome of discriminative *viveka*, a deep understanding of the transience of the world and its phenomenon, it's ultimately unsatisfying nature, and the gentle relinquishment of our obsession with it. It is this cutting-through and cutting-off that can at first blush seem contrary to the loving message of Jesus. But it is this very message that he most powerfully states:

> "Do not suppose that I have come to impose peace upon the earth; I came to impose not peace but a sword. For I came to divide a man against his father, and a daughter against her mother, and a bride against her mother-in-law, and a person's enemies: the members of their household. Whoever cherishes father or mother more than me is not worthy of me; and whoever cherishes son or daughter more than me is not worthy of me. And whoever does not take up their cross and follow after me is not worthy of me. Whoever gains their soul will lose it, and whoever loses their soul for my sake will gain it."

- Matthew 10:34-39

It is this withdrawal or interiorization from the ways that our consciousness diffracts into the form of our organs of perception and action that retraces the steps the One takes in its unfoldment into the many. By cutting through the relative truth with the wonder-sword of discernment that Christ gives, sharpened by the purification of mind - we turn from our habituated modes of seeing and being. Walking back along the path we came, we come to the place of truth and apprehend the pearl of great price that Jesus so powerfully spoke of.

The concrete expression of how this process unfurls is beautifully demonstrated in the Yogic traditions of Hinduism. The various yogas of karma, raja, bhakti and jñana each look very different in isolation - but are simply divergent paths that converge at the same destination, divine Union. Bhakti is the yoga of love and devotion between the lover and Beloved in whatever form stirs that fragrance of intimacy within the heart of the aspirant.

Jñana, on the other hand is the yoga of knowledge and wisdom, but not in solely an intellectual sense. The yoga of knowledge is rightly understood as the direct experience that the Absolute has of itself, and thus is different from bhakti only in form. Both yogas make use of yogic practices like seva, karma, and raja. Seva is the selfless outward activity of service given in love to others for either their material or spiritual benefit. It is the exterior portion of karma yoga, designed to purify our activity in the world.

Karma yoga then in this context is the more interior disidentification with the body and performing all actions as unto the Beloved. It is this modality that serves primarily to purify the heart, or the mind, depending on if we're using western, or eastern terminology. After we have thoroughly purified the heart of projecting happiness on the outside, we come to the regal expression of spiritual practice. Raja is the royal yoga of interiorized spiritual practice and silent meditation where we disidentify ourselves from our minds and rest as silence itself. We may here use the implements of ritual, such as a rosary, an icon, verbal repetition of prayer or mantra, mentally visualized offerings, and simple rest. This mode of practice serves to focus the mind one-pointedly and render it temporarily suspended to dispose us to the influx of divine knowing that is jñana. Of the two paths, bhakti is the more accessible, since we already typically have experienced love and devotion, so it comes naturally to us. There is also nothing to really learn, love is the practice, the goal, and the result. But ultimately it meets back with jñana, because to truly know something, you must love it, and to truly love something, you must know it. That knowing isn't an objective kind of knowledge like *sapientia* or *scientia*, but is an intimate subjective knowing. It's not an I-It relationship where the world of objects seemingly revolves around you as the sole agent, but an I-*Thou* relationship, where all of reality shines with the smile of the infinite. In fact, Pannikar in surgically dividing the Christology of the Church (the study of Christ) from *Christophany* of Christ (the realization of the primordial oneness of the Father with the Son), highlights the macrocosmic reality of that relationship:

"Christophany is an ongoing invitation to realize that we are immersed in and belong to the eternal process of the 'I' 'thou-ing' the Son, a process in which the Spirit urges us to respond with 'Abba, Mother!'"[6] Δ

Beneath the outer layers of our personality rests 'the dignity of our human nature'. The depth of that nature, which can only be given by grace, is revealed when as the anonymous author of the 14th century mystical treatise The Cloud of Unknowing says:

––––––––––––––––––––––––––––––

Δ Panikkar continues, "we might ask ourselves if calling God Father and Mother constitutes an anthropomorphism, or on the contrary, if calling parents Father and Mother might be a theomorphism."

> "Just as this cloud of *unknowing* is above you and between you and your God, it will be necessary for you to put in the same way a cloud of *forgetting* beneath you, between you and all the creatures that have ever been made".[7]

The senses are withdrawn first by act, then by thought, and finally wrought from the will of our small and separate ego self by the continual following after Christ in the radical *kenosis* of our self into emptiness. This *śunyata* really isn't synonymous with nothingness like most people expect. Rather, it is the narrow passageway to fullness. It seems like the cold steel of nihilism from the perspective of the individual, but from the perspective of the absolute, it is the ambrosial kingdom of God. The process of outer discipline in our way of living is directly connected to the interior discipline of the passions, and at a deeper level, the banishing of all images from the intellect and cleaning of the mirror that reflects the pure and flowing light of the Godhead. We must first become still enough to settle the water, so it may faithfully reflect the image of the moon and be made to shine. When we are able to clean the slate the mystics say is truly within us, we are able to obtain that purity of heart with which we see the Divine, for "God is not found in the soul by adding anything, but by a process of subtraction". The Via Negativa, Apophatic theology, and even 'heretical' Quietism are central to the intuitive core of ascetic practice, and the alignment of theory and praxis was the genius of these ancient writers.

When we deny our self and take up our cross, not by punishment, but by love, we take part in a long lineage of finding that there is resurrection on the other side of death, and that the boundaries of our separate sense of self fall away to reveal an interconnection with all of life, and with God. When we reach this realization, even suffering becomes a doorway to release our attachments and to purify our heart in readiness to see the Divine.

The posture of renunciation is indicative of the likeness to Christ, in taking up our cross daily, in releasing of things that no longer serve us, and also in the embracing of gratitude and abundance – letting 'just this' be enough. However, in the end, the only thing we need to truly renounce is wrong-view.

//Meditation//

Now that we have a more solid grasp on what the stage of purgation entails, let's see if we can loosen our grip on everything else.

Find your place to settle and come into your sitting posture. Breathe deep into your nose and out through your mouth a few times until you begin to relax.

Now bring a soft awareness to each of your senses, one at a time. First your sense of sight, then your sense of smell, then your sense of hearing, then your sense of taste, then your sense of touch.

Don't go out into and linger with the objects they're sensing, but just be aware of the sensing itself, without labeling it. If any sense is perceived that pulls you into conceptual rumination, gently withdraw your attention from it. Do this with each sense faculty one by one, until your attention is withdrawn from all of them.

Now close your eyes and let your senses rest.

With your in-breath, notice any interior attachment you might have to objects, events, people, thoughts, feelings, emotions. This can take the form of wanting things to be a certain way, a desire for more, a desire for something better, a desire for something different.

And with your out-breath, let go of absolutely everything. Releasing all the insistencies into space. Breathe in again.

With your out-breath, notice all your aversions and rejections of the reality of what is, in objects, circumstances, people, thoughts, feelings, and emotions. And with the in-breath accept all of those things with an ever-increasing sense of vast spaciousness. Allowing yourself to contain all of it.

"Strive to desire to enter into complete detachment and emptiness and poverty, with respect to everything that is in the world, for Christ.
In order to arrive at having pleasure in everything, Desire to have pleasure in nothing.
In order to arrive at possessing everything, Desire to possess nothing.
In order to arrive at being everything, Desire to be nothing.

In order to arrive at knowing everything, Desire to know
nothing.
In order to arrive at that which you know not, You must go by a
way that you know not.
In order to arrive at that which you possess not, You must go by
a way that you possess not.
In order to arrive at that which you are not,
You must go through that which you are not." [8]

Come back to your breath and express gratitude to God in
whatever form speaks to you. As you go about your day, try to
practice vigilance in closely watching your interior movements of
attachment toward and aversion away from the contents of your
moment-to-moment experience, and observe them with calm
non-attachment, redirecting your desire toward what is.

Part Two:

Moon

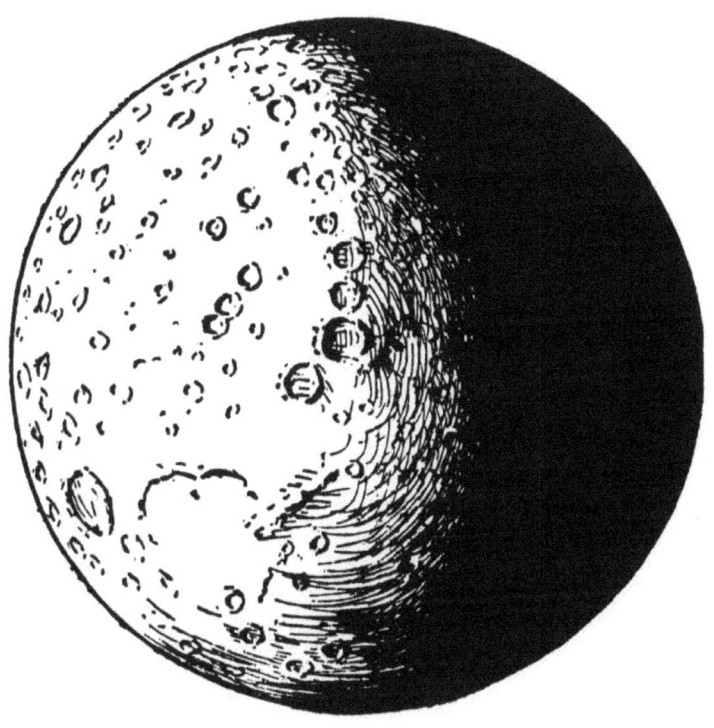

VI

STEPPING OUT OF THE DARK

"It was the true light, which illuminates everyone, that was coming into the cosmos. He was in the cosmos, and through him the cosmos came to be, and the cosmos did not recognize him."

John 1:9-10

Illumination is the stage of our path where we experience the true meaning of contemplation as a long, loving look at the real, a glimpse of reality unfiltered, however fleeting. There are so many mystical itineraries, or outlines of the soul's journey to God that have been sketched out by Saints and mystics through the ages. And they all have their own cultural language, number of stages, and characterization of those stages. Origen, Dionysius, and Gregory of Nyssa had the three we've already spoken of. Some like Saint Bonaventure, built upon this theme to have six stages – after the theophany of St Francis of the six-winged seraphim. He describes these as sensation, imagination, reason, intelligence, understanding, and awareness. Some others like Richard of Saint Victor, describe it in four degrees of violent charity (or unconditional love), characterized by the way desire for the divine increases exponentially as one makes their way on the path. Or Hugh of St. Victor's five forms of divine knowing. Or Marguerite Porete's seven states of being, or possibly the most famous – Teresa of Avila's Seven mansions of the Interior Castle, where she describes the transition from the active acquired contemplation, to passive infused contemplation as mansions in the castle of our soul.

But all these stages are just ways that these travelers before us liked to divide up the one journey that we all embark on into different parts to better understand it. And each journey is unique to every person, their culture, temperament, and conditioning. It's far from linear, and we can go through cycles of these stages, even in reverse order. But there are commonalities in expression for this middle part of the journey that we call illumination.

A WAYPOINT

After spending some time in the dark night of sense, developing that outward detachment from circumstance and form, you may have noticed a deep sense of calm and peace. This is because before purgation, when we place our attention and expectations on the outer world, we try to twist it and bend it to fit our preconceived ideas of what it should be, or what we want. It's an attempt to control the world to suit our individual preferences. But the beautiful thing is, once we engage in purification, and withdraw our attention and expectations from the world of form, we can begin to see it partially as God sees it. We begin to see the divinity baked into every oak tree, every sunset, every child. The paradox is that when we withdraw from the world, we actually begin to see it anew for the first time.

When we stop trying to control the universe, *we set it free.*

It's as if on our journey up the mountain, we had to make our way through a dense thicket of thorns and brush. A path so tangled that we had to strip away some of the heavier things we were carrying just to get through. But after a while, our path opened up to a wide and rolling meadow of soft grasses and floral blossoms. One where we could find rest and recharge ourselves. This sense of peace that arises from not clinging is the aroma of our true nature, drawing us onward and inward.

In a way, that is the first foretaste of illumination, because we are to a degree sampling the fragrance of our true selves united with

God, the flowering fragrance that is love, joy, peace, patience, kindness, goodness, faithfulness, gentleness, and self-control. That first period of illumination shows us that The Spirit of God is within us and guiding us, leading us along our way if we yield to it and direct our desire toward itself only, and not the things of the ego – or the "old man" as Saint Paul referred to his own limited sense of self. This part of the path can be characterized by an emphasis on the aspects of bhakti, and raja yoga – both interiorly orienting ourselves to the divine, and exteriorly relating to our experience as a meeting ground of the Buberian I, and Thou.

This in-itself naturally begins to produce the *Samādiṣatkasampatti,* or the sixfold treasured qualities that characterize a fit student of *atma-jñana,* or self-knowledge in the system of Vedanta. These qualities are the natural result of acute discrimination, and of mature renunciation of the unreality of what typically passes for the world, but we can also intentionally focus on and practice each of them. It begins with the quality of *shama:* the control of our mental faculties by continual meditation on the defects of our objects of desire. When the mind is habitually pulled toward an object via the continuum of attraction or aversion, we bring our attention to the *dosha,* or defects of the object. Not that the object is *bad,* but that it is temporary, fleeting, unsatisfying in any kind of lasting way.

The second quality we cultivate is *dama,* or mastery of the senses. But this restraint of the sense organs is not the same as repression of them. We simply want to be able to reel the mind in from it's preoccupations to focus on our practice without being drawn out by the senses. The next is *uparama,* which is the focusing of the mind and senses that comes about effortlessly as a result of the first two qualifications. Because of this withdrawal of our attention, we are then gifted with *titiksha,* or the forebearance of heat and cold, pleasure and pain, and the other pairs of opposites that arise to inhibit our progress. It is the ability to endure the stresses and trials of life without being knocked too far off course.

Due to the efficacy of the path in uniting the body and the mind, we develop *shraddha* – the faith in the words of the teacher or the scripture. This of course is not a blind faith, but more appropriately a working trust that awaits our own verification. Just as in science class where we are not simply meant to take the instructor's word as the truth, but to independently verify the claims so they become true in our own experience – we are meant to trust the words of our spiritual teachers pending our independent research.

The final quality inculcated is *samadhana*. Samadhana is often translated as the concentration of the mind, but that narrow definition leaves much to be wanted with respect to it's full scope. In a broader context, samadhana is the focusing of our entire lives around the spiritual endeavor. It is the utilization of every facet of our life as fuel in pursuit of our freedom. We no longer have any division between the secular, and the sacred. Instead, our formal spiritual practice seamlessly bleeds out into our everyday life of work, family, friends, and responsibilities.

But these qualities, whether as the fruits of the spirit or the sixfold treasures, are not the final point of our sadhana. The beautiful meadow is just a temporary stop along our greater journey, because our destination is the summit of the mountain itself. These characteristics are given as practices to the seeker, ones where we emulate the aspects of the enlightened being that to them are completely effortless and natural. We begin by deliberately taking inventory of our own capacity with each quality, noticing where we may be too taught, or too loose. And eventually, those qualities which we had to work to embody, become the inherent adornments of our restful being. It is when the cool winds of grace move silently through the sky, and clear away the clouds that the complete orb of the moon can shine.

Teresa of Avila, in her description of the Interior castle describes it as the soul traveling deeper into itself, through the seven mansions of the castle. The first three mansions are primarily active, where the spiritual journey is facilitated by our own cooperation with grace and attaining what she calls acquired contemplation.

But the last four mansions are mainly passive, where God draws the soul into continually deeper stages of union by God's own action in what is sometimes called infused contemplation. The fourth mansion of prayer is referred to as the prayer of quiet, where our exterior sense faculties are quieted in the dark night of sense, and we are absorbed into a deep state of prayer. Our desire is directed toward God in love, but the soul's interior faculties like reason, memory, and understanding normally directed by that desire are left without much to do – so they sort of roam around and can often be a real distraction. It's times like these in our meditation where we find ourselves really centered within ourselves and at peace, but those noisy thoughts keep coming through our minds to try and draw us away. But if we don't allow ourselves to be carried off by our thoughts, what begins to happen according to Teresa, is that a natural spring of water seems to rise from the depth of ourselves, and our soul and awareness seemingly expand to accommodate it.

In the book of Jeremiah, God is referred to as a fountain of living water. And when Jesus speaks to the woman at the well, he references this image of God when he tells her:

> "The water that I will give will become in them a spring of water gushing up to eternal life."

The second part of the path, illumination, also brings with it a piercing truth and clarity, where we can see through the layers of the conditioning of society, and even of our own mind.

In "The Mind's Journey Into God", St Bonaventure says that the Universe itself is a ladder to God. In that we utilize every faculty at our disposal, every joy and every despair, every movement and repose to facilitate our *re-ligio*, our reconnecting to the Divine. He says,

> "We must pass through the vestiges that are corporeal and temporal and outside us; then we must enter into our own mind, which is God's image, everlasting, spiritual, and within us."

This entering into our own mind reveals the ways that our "earthly" or discursive mind is constantly latching onto or pushing away people, things, and events that don't meet its stringent expectations. But we can go even further into our mind and realize that the bulk of our identity is built upon that affective spectrum of attachment and aversion. In a very real way, we *are* our likes and dislikes. We are in a certain sense determined by our attachments and aversions, that unconscious impulse of pushing and pulling is what we typically think makes us "unique" and separates us from everyone else. It forms our very identity.

We are a reasonable person. We're fans of Vivaldi and Dostoyevsky, or maybe Drake and Gillian Flynn. We're influenced by Friedman, or possibly Bakunin. A practitioner of *orthodox* piety and not the heretical new agers. We proudly hold the title of chief thing-doer at our company because of *our* excellent qualities. All these identities are just the shiny packaging around summaries of what parts of reality we accept and reject.

The transient phenomenon we grasp onto to keep our limited identities afloat in the vast ocean of being are the very things that prevent our realization that we *are* that ocean of pure being.

I AM LEGION

There is a multitude within us, all based on scattered desires that branch out from our will, knowledge, and action, veiled by avidya or ignorance.

We try to pick the most socially acceptable version, while the others fester beneath the surface. Or we try to cram all these disparate versions into one cohesive package, but it never works.

Our apparent ignorance of our true nature eventually creates a desire for the Neo-Platonic return of the many to the One.

That restless desire gets misdirected onto things, objects, people, and events - as if they will fulfill us.

Each version of ourselves that we identify with is an amalgamation of attachments and aversions based on that misplaced desire. Each iteration saying confidently, "I am one that lacks X, and will be completed by it."

Part of unraveling the ego is acknowledging these branching patterns of desire, and following them back to their source: desire for Self-knowledge.

Whenever you feel scattered in unmet desires, ask yourself:

Why do I want this?

What desire is *beneath* this object?

Where does this reveal a belief in *lack?*

When you find it, remember that you are that thing in your very being, you've just simply forgotten that aspect of yourself.

Where previously we explored the concept of the dark night of sense, our task now is to go into the second dark night, the dark night of the soul. This is a term you've probably heard in passing, and is often equated with a tough time in life where everything is going wrong, but that isn't what the phrase originally referred to. The dark night of the soul is the darker and more painful part of our journey where we come to grips with our own shadow. Now that the water of our being has had time to settle, the parts of ourselves that we locked away have the chance to bubble up to the surface. Our egoic mind is extremely skilled at maintaining our projected identity to ourselves. So, when we take away the mind's fuel source which is our devoted attention to exterior things, the active ways that the egoic mechanism veils our flaws gradually decelerates.

LOVE AND KNOWLEDGE

The paths of wisdom and love seem different at first, but the methods they use are similar. The wisdom path says God is found in the innermost depths of the soul by subtraction, never addition. Which is why the Vedantic traditions practice the inward path of *neti-neti* (not this not this), and why the Christian monastic tradition practices asceticism or purgation. This doesn't appeal to modern sensibility because we are so overly identified with our bodies and minds that any kind of subtraction is viewed as an attack on our identity. Like that saying 'racism is so American that when you protest it, people think you're protesting America'. But that exclusive identification with the body and mind itself is an attack on our true identity. All the accoutrements we place on top of ourselves serve to mask our insecurity and ignorance. At the bottom of them all is fear and ignorance. The wisdom path removes that fear by removing ignorance and the path of love removes ignorance by removing fear.

Instead of framing it as renunciation for the sake of knowledge, in devotion, it's framed as surrender for the sake of love. That's why Krishna told Arjuna that Bhakti is the easier path for most, because when you truly love someone, giving anything up is the easiest thing in the world. Giving up coffee would be unenjoyable for me, but if my beloved asked me to, it would be nothing at all, even a joy. Because on the path of love, the path is all you need. The love with which you love God is the love with which God loves you. Or in the jñana sense of Meister Eckhart:

> "The eye with which I see God is the eye with which God sees me. One seeing, one knowing, one loving."

Jesus practiced *both*. He went the way of the renunciate through the trials in the desert, the way of wisdom; he also went the way of love. He united both ways and called them his flesh and his blood. We're meant to partake of both.

You may have heard the famous teaching from Nisargadatta Maharaj, "Wisdom tells me I am nothing, Love tells me I am everything, and between the two my life flows." One of the most subtly pervasive problems in the spiritual path is that we often try to be everything without first becoming nothing, expanding our egoic tendencies to encompass the world of our projection. We become liable to get caught on the thorny snares of the world, the impermanence of Buddhism, or what Jesus called building our home on the ever-shifting sands of change. Because really, unless a grain of wheat falls to the ground and dies, it won't produce any fruit.

SHADOW AND PROJECTION

When we encounter some aspect within us that we reject, what tends to happen is that the mind recoils against that feeling of emotional pain, and to protect itself, it hides that aspect of ourselves from us. This is called the shadow. This is why we can't always see our flaws until we enter deeply into silence, stillness, and solitude. Once we have repressed those shadowy parts of ourselves, what then happens is we project those aspects onto others as a way to ensure we won't see them in ourselves.

After all, if the problem is with *them*, it can't be with *me*, right? This is part of the content that the dark night of the soul deals with. In another way, as John of the Cross says, the dark night of the soul is faith itself. It is the darkening of our natural intellect and reason by the brighter light of awareness. Just like when you walk from a dark building into the bright sun, at first you're blinded and can't see anything, the same goes for the dark night of the soul.

Sometimes the incalculable brightness of God blinds us and appears as darkness.

We can't look on it at noon, but have to wait for those liminal and transitory periods. Between the end and the beginning, the good and the bad, the inbreath and the outbreath, the waking and dream states, between the conclusion of one thought and the emergence of another. Then through layers of atmosphere, the sun comes to us in a form we can digest. One that slips through the cracks of our stories like healing balm and *shines* like a ruby in the sky.

God always tells the truth, but like Dickinson – tells it *slant*.

It's as if you were born blind, and someone told you about the color green. You wouldn't really have an understanding of what green is. No matter how much someone told you, you would have to rely on accepting that you don't know experientially. This acceptance is traditionally called unknowing, or faith, but I like to just call it basic trust in reality.

When we first go into this dark night of the soul, it can seem painful on one hand due to what Thomas Keating calls the "unloading of the unconscious", where those stored memories and trauma begin to finally be able to express themselves without the mental resistance of our egoic tendencies pressing down. On the other hand, it can be painful because insofar as we have purified our heart from outward attachments, and directed our desire toward the Divine – it can seem that this desire is withheld from us.

This is because when we typically desire something, we want to intellectually grasp it, but God cannot be known by the mind.

The Kena Upanishad proclaims this truth with piercing clarity:

> "Not that which the eye can see, but that whereby the eye can see: know *that* to be Brahman the eternal, and not what people here adore;
>
> Not that which the ear can hear, but that whereby the ear can hear: know *that* to be Brahman the eternal, and not what people here adore;
>
> Not that which speech can illuminate, but that by which speech can be illuminated: know *that* to be Brahman the eternal, and not what people here adore;
>
> Not that which the mind can think, but that whereby the mind can think: know *that* to be Brahman the eternal, and not what people here adore."

This is why the mystics through the ages have put such an emphasis on the unknowing of God. Because as the anonymous author of the Cloud of Unknowing says -

> "God can be reached and held close by means of love, but by means of thought – *never*."

So, we must rest in this primal desire, and basic trust in God. This rest and trust are deeper and more fundamental than any of our conceptions of God or even the delights that we've experienced in contemplation. It's a rest not in that beautiful meadow we experienced, where the splendor of God was everywhere we looked. But it's a more matured resting in a dryness or aridity without the consolation of spiritual breakthroughs. This is where saint St John of the Cross describes the dark night of the soul as the "narrow road" of the imitation of Christ. Saint John says this:

"Hence it is clearly seen that the soul must not only be disencumbered from that which belongs to the creatures, but likewise, as it travels, must be annihilated and detached from all that belongs to it's spirit."

This non-attachment and emptiness to that which pertains to the understanding and to the spirit is what Jesus called "poverty of spirit". In Matthew 5:3, Jesus says -

> "Blessed are the poor in spirit, for theirs is the Kingdom of God."

This poverty of spirit is equated with the imitation of Christ in his call for us to follow him. Fortunately enough, he tells us precisely how to do this later in the book of Matthew:

> "If any want to become my followers, let them deny themselves and take up their cross and follow me. For those who want to save their life will lose it, and those who lose their life for my sake will find it."

This upside down way of self-surrender is the uncomplicated yoke that Jesus speaks of in Matthew:

> "Take my yoke upon yourselves and learn from me, because I am gentle and accommodating in heart, and you will find rest for your souls; For my yoke is mild and my burden light."

This 'yoke' is the Greek ζυγός - to unite or join, binding tightly together. It is this union that is also the literal translation of the Sanskrit युज्, or *yoga*. John says that on this narrow way, the denial of ourselves which is the cross is not an implement of self-torture, but our walking staff that helps us to reach our destination, and that makes our load not heavier, but lighter. Because in this narrow way, we begin to use the suffering of life as the means for our own awakening. Not seeking to escape it, but to fully embrace the whole of life. So, in this sense, when we can do all things as unto God, we experience the divinity in both joy and in suffering. In this sense, it does almost feel like cheating. But Jesus told us it would feel this way when he says that his yoga is easy, and his burden is light.

The inner tradition of Christianity places a healthy premium on the *via negativa* - the way of descent and purgation into the dark nights of sense and soul that produce the most abject poverty of spirit.

But we can become stuck there, too.

In a liminal threshold between the hell realms of samsāra and the vast expanse of freedom, we can become conditioned into thinking that a state of nothingness, blankness, or listless apathy about the divine is the pinnacle of our quest, and identifying with that state as a perpetual seeker. But this process of unknowing is itself a *pramana*, a means of knowledge that itself falls away in due time.

> "Other indeed is it than the known, and also above the unknown."
>
> Kena Upanishad 1:4

God is beyond the known, and beyond the *unknowing*.

Despite her relative unfamiliarity with forms of spirituality outside the Western sphere of mysticism, Evelyn Underhill in her magnum opus, *Mysticism* speaks well of this:

> "No longer confused by the dim cloud of unknowing, they have pierced to its heart, and there found their goal: that uncreated and energizing fire which guided the children of Israel through the night."

It is not so much that the darkness of learned ignorance occludes our vision. But rather that it is the first intimation of a light which is too bright to see. Meister Eckhart in his timeless way describes this light of knowing:

"Here we must come to a transformed knowledge, and this unknowing must not come from ignorance, but rather from knowing we must get to this unknowing. Then we shall become knowing with divine knowing, and our unknowing will be ennobled and adorned with supernatural knowing."

Meister Eckhart, Sermon Two

But we are not raiding the *mysterium tremendum* like some chilly Prometheus. Mystery doesn't mean you don't know it, but rather that you know it *so* deeply that it renders you completely speechless. You can't say a thing about it because no one thing you could say could encapsulate the depth of that peerless truth. We must ultimately proceed from the mistaken knowledge that the world, and God are somewhere 'out there' at a distance from us, and we are 'in here' (here being the physical body). Leaving this mistaken knowledge behind, we come to the *parokśa jñana*, or indirect knowledge of Reality given through the words of scripture and the living teacher. That mediated knowledge itself, once it dissolves any remnants of dualistic knowledge, leads to a complete unknowing of all things. This unknowability is simply a pointer to go beyond the duality of knowing and unknowing entirely. It is the utterly ungraspable nature that makes all else knowable. The only kind of knowledge applicable to God's essence is Self-Knowledge. God is unknowable for the very reason that the eye is unseeable. The Divine cannot be an object to Herself because She is endlessly pure and limitless awareness. The precursory unknowing is not so much a 'not seeing' in the ultimate sense, but more accurately a *seeing through* of the phenomenon of existence. And what is it that we see through to? The *aparokśa jñana* or unmediated and pristine supernatural knowing that God has of Herself:

I

The most esoteric form of knowing has nothing to do with knowledge as we conventionally define it, but it has everything to do with *love*. Because when everything is apprehended not just theoretically, but directly as our very Self, who will we hate?

The most mystical experience, or the most profound state of samādhi isn't really an experience or state at all. The deepest transformation is to change *nothing*, because it's our incessant need to continually engage in performative violence over the non-dual field of Reality that drives the desire for transformation to begin with. And the most radical expression of faith is to not reject anything whatsoever, knowing that all that is – is the Real.

Whether it's called transformation or spiritual growth, seeking a change in extrinsic stimuli or intrinsic responses can be a subtle way of spiritual escapism. It can rouse us out of inertiatic tamas, into the movement of rajas, and to the stillness of inner peace. But the more we open our eyes to grace, the less important it becomes to change anything.

Counterintuitively, it is when we can accept the world, as well as our full humanity with all its sandpaper that we're able to fully embody the divinity that gives shape to the silk of Reality.

No matter what the means of practice is, the end arrives of its own accord. The deeper transformation or alignment of Will is only natural and lasting when it's born out of a clear seeing. In the acceptance of all things as they are, including the things we want to transform, the desire to transform and the transforming itself are all equally expressions of the Real.

// Meditation //

This meditation is based on what we've explored in our contemplative journey so far, based in part by the words of Christ in scripture, the light of reason in St. John, and the witness of tradition in The Cloud of Unknowing. The last wheel on our vehicle therefore is one of experience, which only you can provide.

So, settle into your contemplative prayer position, whether that's sitting on the edge of a chair, or on the floor with your legs crossed.

Bring your attention to your breath and watch it naturally flow in and out a few times until the body and mind come to rest in equanimity.

Now as any exterior sounds, smells, or other sensations arise, simply withdraw your attention from them completely.

Place a thick cloud of forgetting between them and yourself.

There may be particularly loud or potent distractions that may try to assault you, and they may try to break through that cloud.

But your attention and desire is completely withdrawn from them, so their strength doesn't really move you away from the centerpoint of stillness in the innermost cave of your heart. Place again that cloud of forgetting between you and everything both beneath and outside of you.

Now likewise, as any interior thoughts, images, concepts, feelings, emotions, or insights arise, place a cloud of forgetting between them as well.

No matter how alluring or divine the thought or image may seem, it isn't what you're here for. So simply allow it to gently pass by you.

And finally, place a cloud of complete unknowing between you and God. Because God cannot be grasped by the mind.
The more we recline into our basic trust of God, not trying to fit Her into our heads, the more of Her is revealed to us within the depths of our heart.

Direct a completely open and naked intent toward the Divine.

Anytime an exterior or interior thing auditions for your attention, simply let that cloud of forgetting to envelop it.

And anytime you feel your rational mind trying to dissect or understand God or what you're experiencing in this prayer, let the cloud of unknowing swallow it whole.

And again, and again return to that *piercing dart of love* toward God as a wordless movement within the cave of the heart.

Slowly bring your attention back into the room, and move your body around a little bit.

See if you can stay relaxed into that sense of pure love toward the unknown throughout all the comings and goings of your day.

When frustration arises: *forgetting*.

When attachment arises: *unknowing*.

When nothing in particular arises: *rest*.

VII

THE BRIDAL CHAMBER

पश्यामि त्वां दीप्तहुताशवक्त्रं-
स्वतेजसा विश्वमिदं तपन्तम्॥ ११॥

anādi-madhyāntam-anantavīryam- ananta-bāhum śaśi-sūrya-netram, paśyāmi tvām dīpta-hutāśa-vaktram- svatejasā viśvam-idam tapantam.

"I see You without beginning, middle, or end, infinite in power, of endless arms, the sun and moon being Your eyes, the burning fire Your mouth, heating the whole universe with Your radiance."
The Song of the Lord 11:19

The writings of the tradition attest that the supreme goal of the Christian life is to have lasting and transformative Divine Union. The desire for this freedom, called *mumukshutva* is the all-consuming desire to finally become what we already are. This Union, or *deification* put simply is the process of becoming transformed into God. This will probably sound heretical and preposterous to modern western seekers that were given an image of God being outside, untouchable, and distant. But this isn't the God spoken about by Jesus. That God was Abba, Father. A term of intimacy that could have been dangerous in his day as well. And Abba wasn't just *his* Father, because in the verbal prayer modeled by Jesus, he begins with "Our Father" or as Rob Bell says - *Father of us*. As in you, me, and everyone and everything. The word itself not only implies a relationality, but an *identity* and *authority*.

Jesus lived from that state of union with God. Exemplified by his statement in John 14:9 when he says:

"Whoever has seen me, has seen the Father."

Some of the first scriptural references for our own uniting with God were ones like 1 Corinthians 6:17 "Anyone united to the Lord becomes *one spirit* with Him."

This passage is used by Saints like Macarius of Egypt and Bernard of Clairvaux to describe a uniting of two natures, human and divine within one body, in a way similar to Christ. In this union, the human will is fused with the divine will in love, making it so that their own will is emptied of personal desire completely. This then has the effect of making anything the person wills to be in harmonious concert with the will of God. This fusion of wills is reflected in John 5:19 when Christ says:

> "Very truly, I tell you, the Son can do nothing on his own, but only what he sees the Father doing; for whatever the Father does, the Son does likewise."

It is this surrendering of our will to God above the level of our senses and our spiritual faculties that gives us true freedom. Free will in this sense, isn't just doing what we want, but simply wanting what *is* insofar as it is reflective of the beatitude of God. John Ruysbroeck describes this willing unity as our enlightened sharing in the loving embrace of the Trinity. When this happens, he says those souls that have been illumined by the radiant love of God are "lifted up with free mind above reason to a bare vision devoid of images. There lives the eternal invitation of God's unity, and with imageless naked understanding they go beyond *all* works, and *all* practices, and *all* things, to the summit of their spirit."
John Ruuysbroeck, *Adornment of the Spiritual Marriage*

An analogy that's used in the writings of the mystics is one of air on a sunny day being transformed into sunshine itself, instead of being lit up. Or how iron when heated in a furnace takes on the nature of the fire itself. And how a drop of water seems to completely disappear into a bottle of wine, even taking on the wine's taste and color. That water is our individual will, and the bottomless ocean of wine, the love of God.

It's the same thing in our journey when all our human feelings seem to mysteriously melt away and flow into that love. This can be perceived as an incredible bliss, or as simple contemplation in an imageless emptiness, devoid of all except that awareness of the divine.

In The Interior Castle, St. Teresa describes this stage as the prayer of union, where God begins to still our soul's interior faculties and suspends them in a similar way to our senses, so that both exterior and interior perception is completely darkened, and we rest in that completely naked unknowing. After this experience of the fifth mansion, we find ourselves desiring silence or meditation even more, wanting to return again and again to that interior state of tranquillity.

Mansion six is what is called the room of spiritual betrothal. In this stage, Teresa describes it as complete absorption, where God unites with us, but in a way we can't fully perceive yet. She says that during that moment of union, we don't really even feel anything because we are in complete stillness. We may only reflect after the fact of what may have happened in our prayer period. These are those beautiful times of meditation when we sit for twenty or thirty minutes, but it only feels like 30 seconds. This is because time is typically experienced as the measured flow of objects of perception. And when our interior faculties of attention and perception are withdrawn from objects and concepts, there seems to be no perception of time. The effect of this kind of prayer can last longer than just the sitting period, but seems to permeate that sense of peace into your daily life, for days or weeks at a time.

Finally, God places the soul in the very center of herself, which is God's own dwelling place – The Bridal Chamber. Teresa describes this, "as two whose lives are so intertwined nothing could ever separate them."

This unification of our identity is when the entirety of our being, including our faculties and our will are subsumed into God and united with Her. Then we can truly say -

"Not my will, but *Yours*."

This is when it becomes our will to do the will of God, and where we cease to want to do otherwise. It is when we begin to resemble not just the Image of God in our particular incarnation, in our contemplative being, but also the likeness of God, in our becoming, our action. It is when we mimic the act of Christ's *kenosis* – the complete emptying of ourselves that we become like God, because that self-emptying is the nature of God emptying into Christ, and Christ emptying into the Holy Spirit, and the Holy Spirit emptying into our own being. We become part of the *perichoresis* or the circle-dance of the Trinity, as we have become pure vessels for God to dwell within. In this stage of meditation, there isn't awareness of the soul within the body, because there is no awareness of soul or body, there is simply *spirit*.

At first this comes as an experience in a particular location and a particular time. We may have a 'mystical experience' in prayer, or in nature, or in a time of great love or great suffering. We might associate this with a particular spiritual practice, or an especially thin place in the world, or a saintly person, or a profound book with that experience. We may build an altar of sorts to that place within our mind, continually coming back to it to try and regain that sense of illumination or union. We think that whatever it was that mediated that experience within us contains the experience itself.

But we're just chasing a memory.

That illumination, that Union is within our very being itself. In fact, it *is* our very being itself. That's all the spiritual or contemplative journey is really, it's a coming back home to who we really are. And who we really are is one with God.

But still, we go through this period of spiritual oscillation, where we alternate between states of illumination and darkening, of spiritual highs and spiritual lows. We might have a period of prayer or meditation where our mind is completely still and peaceful, or our heart is *bursting* with bliss and love, and then the next day, it's like we have a monkey on a drum set between our ears.

It can be tempting to focus on that blissful state we experienced before, but *all experience is a trap in some sense.*

What we want in this state isn't necessarily the Divine, but the peaceful feeling we get from meditative prayer. We oscillate because we still have a spatial-temporal perception of the Divine.

We repent, or go through a *metanoia* of going beyond the mind, and in this we change where we look for happiness - from outward material things, inward to emotional experiences. But John of the Cross says there are many that don't ever even receive spiritual consolation from God. Some people get invited up the front entrance, where they receive consolation, and peace, and bliss, and visions, and ecstasies. But some get invited up the back staircase, where they are lifted up in complete darkness, being completely oblivious to their soul's travel. And so, these beautiful experiences are not even necessary for divine union but are a pure gift. He also advocates for us to practice in contemplative prayer a pure faith that goes beyond what we may or may not experience of God, to God's own S*elf.* Essentially, it is trusting with the core of our very being that *even if we have no experience whatsoever*, that God is working within us and through us.

But after we continually mimic the cruciform nature within contemplative prayer, this place of peace becomes not something we go *to*, but something we come *from*. Then the oscillation ceases, and we are sanctified in lasting union with God.

The spiritual marriage in this sense is like rain falling from the sky into a river, there is nothing but water. Or like a little stream flowing into the ocean, how would you begin to separate them out again? We are able to consistently maintain awareness of God's presence and action within our own being, as well as God's presence and action in everything that exists. We are able to see the timeless quality of existence, as well as the interconnection of all spatial elements. In ourselves, we see not just who we are now, but our entire journey including the trials and sufferings that made us into who we are. Once we perceive this in ourselves, it becomes much easier to perceive it in others as well. We first perceive God within our very selves, then within everyone else – including our enemies. The Divine is seen *within* all that exists, and yet also *containing* all that exists.

Temples within temples within temples.

Father Thomas Keating calls this the "transsubjective communion of love" and it is here where we have our transfiguration of consciousness. An upgrade of our software so to speak. We "put on the mind of Christ", as Paul says, through the going beyond our own mind. The mind of Christ in truth cannot be put on. Rather it is revealed in the shedding of our ordinary mind. It is *revealed* when our habitual ignorance, attachment, and aversion is sublimated into God's own life. Thomas Merton describes it like this -

"In Louisville, at the corner of Fourth and Walnut, in the center of the shopping district, I was suddenly overwhelmed with the realization that I loved all these people, that they were mine and I theirs, that we could not be alien to one another even though we were total strangers. It was like waking from a dream of separateness, of spurious self-isolation in a special world. . . .

This sense of liberation from an illusory difference was such a relief and such a joy to me that I almost laughed out loud. . . . I have the immense joy of being man, a member of a race in which God Himself became incarnate. As if the sorrows and stupidities of the human condition could overwhelm me, now that I realize what we all are. And if only everybody could realize this! But it cannot be explained. There is no way of telling people that they are all walking around shining like the sun.

Then it was as if I suddenly saw the secret beauty of their hearts, the depths of their hearts where neither sin nor desire nor self-knowledge can reach, the core of their reality, the person that each one is in God's eyes. If only they could all see themselves as they really are. If only we could see each other that way all the time. There would be no more war, no more hatred, no more cruelty, no more greed. . . . But this cannot be seen, only believed and 'understood' by a peculiar gift."

This is the essence of the Divine Marriage, the transforming of our relationship to everything. We could spend our whole lives at this stage, and many people spend their whole lives seeking for it.

But there's a second type of union that has an even deeper trajectory, into the non-dual, the not-two. But to get to this final Union, we must go through the third Dark Night, which is the darkest of all. The dark night of Self.

In the first type of Union, there is still a separate sense of self to be united with God. And afterward, there's a self to recognize its union. If Union between two disparate natures is possible, then separation must be the state we're looking from. This is where the path of jñana yoga becomes paramount, where the former posture of I-It, and even I-Thou become sublimated into *I-I*. We see that who we truly are isn't the body, the mind, or even the soul; our true identity is one that not only never dies, but is *ajati – unborn*. We see the face of emptiness directly in the recognition that when we look behind our eyes -

There's nobody there.

The ego, or 'small self' as most spiritual teachers describe it, is not really an entity as much as it is the activity of claiming or identification. It is the clown that takes a bow at the end of the play he wasn't even in. It is not a being, but a *doing*. Often in spiritual circles the concept gets repeated of a 'small self' and a 'higher self'. The small self being the rendition of 'you' that is confined and triggered by the world and its miseries, and the higher self being the you that somehow transcends all of that. We're told to commune with our higher self, while further showing compassion to our lower self.

Sometimes this can help us untangle ourselves from our accumulated layers of identity. Other times, it can usher in a more subtle film across the lens. We can become identified with the role of the yogi, the contemplative, the seeker, or even the 'finder'. But if we remain open and curious, we eventually begin to investigate the validity of this self that seems to be stretched between the divergent poles of waking up and going back to sleep. The one to whom both the lower, and the higher self appear as objects of cognition. And what we end up finding is that separating our identity into lower and higher only further serves to divorce our sense of being from its natural indistinction from reality. Ultimately, we don't need to ascend, descend, or transcend. We need not embody, integrate, or mediate. All that's required is that we remove the obscurations that *seem* to conceal the ever-present truth.

Truly, you have no 'higher self', *no lower one either.*

The Buddhist conception of *anatman*, or not-self is not contested in the Vedic conception of *Atman*, contrary to popular belief. Whether we call our outer garments 'heaps', or 'sheaths' matters very little in the end. What does matter is that we by simple insight relinquish the things that seem to veil our naked being, to discover the simplicity of natural presence that is always already there.

The mind of Christ is not a particular *kind* of consciousness, but Consciousness *itself.*

One of the most important questions Jesus repeats throughout the gospels is,

"Who do you say that I Am?"

Some of his followers thought he was the sequel to the Maccabean revolution, one who would lead them by violent rebellion to political independence from Greek and Roman rule.

Others said he was a divine prophet, akin to Elijah - calling the people back to covenant purity.

Some said he was the *gardener.*

In John's gospel, we get a more esoteric taste of the identity of Christ. He proclaims to be the bread of life, the light of the world, the gate, the good shepherd, the vine, the way, the truth, the resurrection, the life.

But in his characteristic boldness, at one point he dropped all the qualifiers to say simply,

"I Am."

And who are *you*, when you drop all your qualifiers? Who are *you* in the midst of bitter suffering and ecstatic jubilation? What is the most basic thing you can say about *your* self?

I Am.

I Am.

I Am.

God's love affair with you is consummated in the intimacy of the knowledge, "I Am." Swami Abhishektananda, a pioneer of Christian-Hindu dialogue goes so far as to say that, "The discovery of Christ's 'I Am' is the ruin of any Christian theology, for all notions are burnt within the fire of experience."

Because however much of our experience has this sense of otherness, this feeling of distinction between ourselves and the Real, we haven't fully gone to the peak of our contemplative journey. Our very reality, our true being, is concealed in what looks like absolute zero. What we aren't, the small separate sense of self, seems to be real, and what we really are seems to be unreal. It's fully within our strength to expose this imposter and recover our true identity. And the way to this truth is the path of descent and kenosis, which brings us to reject the illusory phantom that dresses in your clothes and accept the basic presence that is nothing all that special to us or anyone else but is our true reality in the eyes of the Divine. This most interior self is well past the myopic wanting and enjoying of the creature the world seems to encourage. As long as we experience ourselves in prayer as the "one who prays", an individual "Me" reaching out, waiting to receive something from Her, we're still a long way from the shores of pure contemplation.

From our perspective it's like we're standing on the edge of a cliff with no railing. We can't seem to get closer, even though we want to, even though it scares us. But the reason is perhaps that there is also no chasm. The next stirring is a moveless progress.

You don't go from one stage of prayer to the next.

What happens is that the separate being that you believe to be you apparently vanishes.

Our projection of our nature into an ideal form for the coming into resonance of our cooperation with reality is really the invisible hand of grace drawing all things to Herself. She gives us a target to focus on and to stop obsessing over our smallness, and then She blurs into the background.

And all that's left is love loving love.

And then nothing's happening anymore.

It's just *this*.

// Meditation //

Let's take that next step of nothing together.

Find somewhere to sit and settle yourself briefly.

Bring your attention to your breath.

Allow it to flow in and out through your nose or mouth in a natural way.

Soft, unforced.

You're not doing it, it's happening by itself.

It's being done *unto* you.

When you're not concentrating on breathing, *who breathes for you?*

When you forget to beat your own heart, *what keeps it going?*

When you aren't trying to think about anything, don't thoughts happen anyway?

145

It's all on automatic.

The same goes with our spiritual path.

That desire that you think you have for peace, for love, for God?

That's God desiring *within* you.

Even the most noble and pure thing we think about ourselves, our connection to spirit, is really just spirits connection to spirit. We don't have much to do with it.

We just need to relax and get out of the way.

With that spirit of absolute surrender, sink beneath the flow of your thoughts and emotions like a stone into the depth of your being, that is always and already one with God.

There is not now, nor has there ever been a speck of distance between the fullness of God's being and our own.

Every bit of it too close to say, 'here'.

Anytime you feel a doubt or fear creeping in, recognize it as simply coming from a habitual sense of separation. From the false self-system that we've been practicing our whole life. And allow the tension from that mistaken sense of self to dissipate into that deep rest of who you really are.

Open your eyes.

Go about your day with this truth reverberating through the halls of your heart, that there is no separation from God whatsoever except what we fabricate in our minds from fear of losing a self that doesn't even really exist.

VIII

MODERN DAY MYSTICISM

"You are the light of the world. A city set upon a hill cannot be hidden; Neither do they light a lamp and place it under the dry-goods basket, but rather they place it upon a lampstand, and it illumines all who are in the house. So let your light shine out before humanity, so that they may see your good works and may glorify your Father in the heavens."

Matthew 5:14-16

We don't need to live in an Egyptian desert, or in a cave in the Himalayas to recognize and participate in the reality of Spirit. So how do we maintain authenticity and dedication to the Divine amidst the hustle and bustle of everyday existence? How do we abide with, in, and *as* our True Self in the chaos of so many false selves?

The contemplative journey I'm presenting here isn't necessarily a linear path. Sometimes we have to go two steps forward, and one step back. Often, we get to what we think is the end of the path, when it's actually just the beginning. You might have had this feeling hiking on a long trail, feeling like you've reached the destination only to realize it's just a bend in the continuing path. Or sometimes, we even experience the same thing again because we're going in circles. The nature of the contemplative journey is one of a descending spiral. We're always being invited to go deeper, and we might experience things we've already been through, only this time one level down.

We travel through the dense thorns of purgation, letting go of our attachments to exterior things and directing our desire for wholeness and completion inward toward ourselves and the divine. We surrender our attachment to the body, our over-identification with it, and our outward sense faculties that promise us fulfilment.

We experience the prayer of recollection, in those rare moments where we seem to be whisked into silence, stillness, and solitude before being spit back out into the world of chaos. We struggle through the dark night of sense where we may have lost some of the former consolation of our prayer life. We develop a sense of detachment from the ups and downs of our affective emotions, attachments and aversions. We reach an alpine meadow full of the sweet fragrance of inner peace and unconditioned joy that gives us refreshment and spurs us onward and inward.

Here we are able to attain to the prayer of quiet, where our outer faculties are suspended, or will and desire absorbed in God, and our imagination, reason, and memory sometimes running amok. We persevere through the dark night of the soul, now seeing the ways in which our projections and attachments cover over who we really are, and separate us from ourselves and others. We battle the spiritual ego, one that desires the things of God but not God Herself. One that prides itself on being more "advanced" in the journey or the most humble. We deal with spiritual oscillation due to an unclear spatial and temporal perception of God. And finally, we climb the final ascent to the summit of Divine Union in two forms, the dualistic, and the non-dual – realizing God within us, Us within God, and then transcending any separation whatsoever.

But we can't stay on the mountain forever. We ultimately have to come back down from the high peak of contemplation and back into the active life, right?

But the life of Mary and Martha aren't opposites.

Contemplation and action aren't opposing strategies for how to live.

Sure, on one level, we engage in prayer and meditation, maybe experience the gifts of contemplation. Then we go to our job or take care of the kids, mow the lawn.

But this perception is still one of separation. If this is how we perceive our life – periods of "spiritual stuff" and wide swaths of "secular stuff" then we're still seeing with a dualistic lens. It's this oscillation that I mentioned in the last chapter. But this is just the sixth mansion, the stage of spiritual betrothal. Because the prayer of full union in the divine marriage slowly or all at once does something to us. It changes the way we see *everything*.

Then there's no oscillation because we know deep in our bones that there can truly be no separation from God, and that any thought that appears otherwise, is simply a lie born of fear. Then there is no profane, *there is only the sacred*.

This is crucial to understand because many people tend to go to a retreat or seminar, have an experience of awakening, and then think all the work is done and over with. But this is just when the work gets difficult. They think they've been "enlightened" simply because they've had an experience of illumination. Often, it's this illumination that shows us where the work still needs to be done. It shows us the ways in which our ego can become a type of spiritualized ego, where instead of using wisdom to be free of our false self, it is used to aggrandize it.

You'll have acquired a deep peace, a detachment from outer circumstances, and cultivated a loving devotion to God, then all of the sudden, your ego taps you on the shoulder and says, "That's very nice, well done!" That's why many masters will discourage the reading of spiritual texts at a certain stage and say that praxis will always win over theory. Knowing about Union with God and experiencing it are two completely different things. The map is not the territory, and the menu is not the dish.

So how do we develop that practice?

First of all, wherever we are on our journey, we have to be honest with ourselves. Look at the broad overview of the path and its stages, how the mystics like John of the Cross or Teresa of Avila describe them and examine what resonates with you.

If you're just starting out, a dedicated silent prayer or meditation practice is crucial. It's a way of de-programming ourselves from our old operating system and its programs for happiness and allowing a fresh install to be "transformed by the renewing of our mind." A daily twenty-minute sit helps sever the ties to our drives for safety and security, affection and esteem, or power and control. It helps establish that deep center of contemplation that carries us through our active lives. And this habit can still be a component if you're farther along in your journey. But the difference is monumental.

Much of the time, meditation can be consumed by thoughts of doing.
Am I doing this right?

Is this even doing anything?

I should be doing something more productive right now.

But meditation is less of a *doing,* and more of a *being.*

It's the refusal to let our identity be sliced up into pieces and thrown to the world to devour. It's a relaxing back into the reality of our own being, ever still, ever pure, *ever shining.*

In his *Upadshasahasri*, Adi Śankara thunders, "I am of the nature of *nirvikalpa*", signifying that pristine meditative absorption where all the waves of the mind cease, and the ego and its mental and emotional impressions sublimate into pure bliss.

So don't worry about whether you're 'doing meditation correctly' because truly, *you already are that*.

Instead of *doing* contemplative prayer to become filled or transformed with divine peace, you discover that the very *nature* of your being is prayer, and peace is the fragrance of that true nature. Then meditation becomes not something you *do*, but something you *are*. Then there's no difference between your silent twenty-minute centering prayer, and your driving to work, or making dinner. This is the true meaning of praying without ceasing.

We begin to see that the posture of stillness is still available within our active life, and we can use the circumstances and events of life as fuel for our further transformation. We can be in conversation with someone, and drop into that open spaciousness of heart, where we're not simply waiting for our turn to speak, not thinking out what we want to say, but also not simply listening to the content of the words spoken. We can listen deeply to the hopes, desires, pain, and suffering of the other person that lies behind the words. We can see them as images of God, not just theoretically, but *experientially* as God coming to us in that moment to open our heart to what is.

Often in post-Christian or ex-evangelical culture, there's a strong emphasis on social justice, economic equity, and environmental restoration. Largely this seems to be a result of such great suffering in the world that it lights a fire of compassion within us to reach out. But equally as often, we can get so focused on being the one that is helping that we don't actually do that much to help. Being the "progressive" Christian can be a way for our spiritual ego to hide within action as a way of proving its worth and prolonging its life. We can then hate and denigrate those that do not think like us – mirroring the abusive culture we thought we escaped.

Or we may have no overtly harmful projections, but we are so attached to the fruit of our actions, that we get burnt out when we try to "do" justice. We get outraged at the injustice of the world, then we get fired up and rush in to make change, often not understanding the nature of what we're getting into. We can often get sucked into playing the role of the savior, having all the answers to solve the world's problems. Then we put all of our energy and time into fixing the problem, and when it doesn't work, we get discouraged and give up.

This is where most contemporary teachers come in and say that we need to temper our action with contemplation. That even Jesus had to separate from the crowd to be alone. And this is true on one level, but on another, it's just a dualistic perception of contemplation.

The union of action and contemplation isn't one of oscillation, of one then the other. The union of action and contemplation is *contemplative action*. As the Gospel of Thomas says, the sign of the Father in us is movement, and repose. It's letting the work of service be done *through* you, not *by* you.

> "Those who see action in inaction and inaction in action are truly wise amongst humans."
> Bhagavad Gita 4:18

It is this enactment of karma yoga that comprises the surrendering the fruit of your efforts to the Divine. The metaphoric field of the battle of our experience, *kshetra*, is symbolic of the entirety of *prakriti*, or nature. While the knower of the field, represented by Krishna, is the subject to whom all objects appear. This epic battle plays out in our lives in myriad ways, one of which is how we engage in action.

In the above passage, Krishna describes how to the wise, much of our rushing around doesn't actually accomplish much. We travel here and there to acquire this and accomplish that, but how much of it ever lasts?

He also reveals the emptiness of "doing meditation" as just more action for results in the midst of inaction. Krishna goes on to say that it's when we're free from the anxiety about results, having already been fulfilled by knowledge of our true identity that we are able to show the sign of "movement and repose" in all actions. That until we renounce the fruit of our endeavors, knowing that we are already fulfilled, we're really just spinning our wheels.

In a deeper way, it can be thought of as non-action, or what the Taoist tradition calls *wu-wei*. And that might have a negative connotation, but non-action is not inaction. It is simply a way of saying that there's no individual sense of doership in what you're doing. There's no drive for affection, security, or control in your service to others, but it, like stillness and peace, is simply an extension of who you are.

Then it's not *you* giving food to the hungry, it's just the food moving from here to there. Then it's no longer *you* calling your senator to oppose legislation that disproportionately harms at-risk communities, but the calling is just what's happening, and you're aware of it all going by.

And with no one doing the work, the work happens by itself. And then who is there to be tired? Who is there to be discouraged? To give up?

It all can be summarized in the call of Jesus to be "in the world, but not of the world." And it is not just for the yogi to recognize their own non-doership, but simultaneously the non-doership of all others. If by spiritual insight we apprehend that we are the unattached witness of all action, but still perceive other beings to be the locus of their action, we have greatly misunderstood. We must not only see how our own bodies and minds are moved by our conditioning, and the force of the past, but that the same is true for everyone else. This is no small point, because once it is directly seen that even the most reprehensible people are simply being blown by the wind of their past action and their current level of mind, we can begin to become a true vector for compassion. In truth, everyone (including you) is completely innocent. It is with this mindset that Jesus on the cross says:

"Father, forgive them; for they do not know what they are doing."
Luke 23:34

The Ultimate gift of compassion to the world is demanding nothing of it. This is the crucial key to our path down the mountain. That we let the suffering of the world open our heart, but we do what we do as if it's all an act of worship to the Divine. That we watch the whole display with unbearable compassion. That's the spiritual technology of forgiveness. And the great thing about forgiving reality for what it is, is that when we drop our filters, it stands revealed as one end of a dynamic and flowing unity.

To know completely is to become knowledge, to love completely is to be utterly *dissolved* in love itself.

// Meditation //

Find somewhere to sit where you won't be disturbed.
Settle briefly and place your attention on that naked intent to surrender to the Divine.

Let everything else fall away.

Allow your body to be still, allow your breath to continue naturally, allow your thoughts to come up as they please.

Center on your desire for God. Or rather, God's desire within you.

Now consciously bring to mind a time when you may have done something that wasn't reflective of your true nature. Something that maybe wasn't loving or peaceful. Something that might stimulate feelings of guilt or shame.

Don't begin to fall into habitual judgement of yourself for it. That guilt that we feel is just another way for the ego to latch onto us.

Gently cradle that thing within the open space of awareness, and simultaneously open your heart to the love the Divine has for you.

Even beyond the things you may have done or thought in an unloving way, the Beloved looks at you and says, "*Forgive them, they know not what they do*".

Everything contrary to love that you've done is because of the conditioning of your life, and the belief in a mistaken idea of who you are.

You literally *couldn't* have done better because you didn't *know* better. Showing yourself that compassion isn't an elusion, it's a way to bring awareness to the shadowed aspects of our activity and integrate them into a larger and more unified space.

Guilting yourself just pushes it further and further out of your perception where it can mutate, metastasize, and control your behavior.

Instead of listening to the words of others, or our own internalized self-hatred, allow God's word about you to be true, that you are innocent of the things you've done because you were asleep to your true nature.

Rest in that healing balm of forgiveness.

Not as an overlooking of what's happened, but in an acknowledgement that your true self in union with God cannot sin, and any mistake you made was one of misplaced identity. Note too that this forgiveness is given to the entire world, to all of reality.

Bring your attention back to the room. As you go about your day in the coming weeks, I encourage you to bring this method into your daily life.

When someone cuts you off in traffic, when your loved one makes a poor decision, when you find yourself judging, thinking of the ways that you would have done things differently – look on them and yourself with the compassion of God. And practice forgiveness knowing that everyone is innocent, because anything they do contrary to love is because they are asleep to their true nature that *is* love. And allow that recognition of absolute forgiveness to ignite that vast and spacious love within yourself *as* yourself. That holy openness then has the capacity to radiate and warm that person, mirroring to them their own true nature that is of the very self-same love.

Part Three:

Sun

IX

DIFFRACTION

ॐ पूर्णमदः पूर्णमिदं पूर्णात्पूर्णमुदच्यते ।
पूर्णस्य पूर्णमादाय पूर्णमेवावशिष्यते ॥
ॐ शान्तिः शान्तिः शान्तिः ॥

om pūrnamadah pūrnamidam pūrnātpūrnamudacyate |
pūrnasya pūrnamādāya pūrnamevāvaśiṣyate | |
om śānti śānti śāntih | |

"The fullness is the Reality. The fullness is all This. From fullness this fullness has issued forth. Taking fullness from fullness, what remains is fullness."

- Isavasya Upanishad 1.1

We often confuse our metaphysics for our experience. That's the tragic history of much of the Church. Forming abstract ontological and cosmological doctrine violently divorced from life, hopelessly academic, theologians would often mistake a description of objective reality, with the reality of direct experience. Cynthia Bourgeault calls it, "the conflation of eternal principle and temporal process."[9] I in no way aim to develop here a novel or corrective metaphysic of the triune nature. I am under no *Robertsian* delusion that I alone have discovered the true Christ, and all the pitiable souls who came before were tragically mistaken. It is simply that no examination of Christian *darśana*[2] would be adequate without a mention of its most notable pedagogical tool. Because truly, the only division to be spoken of in the indivisible Godhead is the one we artificially superimpose with our minds. And so, the Trinity in all its dynamic beauty is most accurately seen as a didactic mechanism by which the great souls of the past have reified their numinous experience as a bridge by which to bring us to the sacred knowledge they have embodied.

While the vehicle of myth and story serve to deliver us timeless truth in the guise of time by working *beneath* the rational intellect in our subconscious tendencies – the mediums of metaphysics,

---

[2] Darśana is a word in dharmic traditions to refer to a 'view' of the Divine. Although sometimes used to refer to brief glimpses of deities, in the broader context it refers to the defining wisdom arising from the direct experience of Reality. A corollary here would be the esoteric pinnacle of gnosis, or the sophianic aspect of philosophy.

cosmology, and theology can more often than not act as a barrier to true understanding by transforming the most intimate aspects of our experience into concepts to be held at arms-length.

THE TRIUNE GOD

Metaphysical models themselves begin from, and end in a place of subject and object distinction, they seldom reveal non-dual truth. But the expression we know as the Trinity, was primarily meant to be an illustration of the path of our experience. It isn't meant to be solely examined analytically, but to be *lived*.

Still, to be useful to us as a model of reality it must be at least modestly understood. The trinity is not of much use to us if approached from the typical standpoint of, 'Just don't think about it, it isn't meant to be understood.' Because if the symbol has no explanatory power, then holding onto it might be limiting our expression to create new symbols of meaning that help move us from living a life characterized by suffering to one defined by liberation. The denigration of the intellect, a valid instrument for the removal of our ignorance from the basecamp of the spiritual path, is unfortunate, especially since according to most maps, the intellect or *buddhi* is the most proximate aspect to our source.

Although the intellect itself must be ultimately transcended, to do so prematurely would be like abandoning your boat and wading into the waves, since the vessel is of no use on the destination of the distant shore.

First, as most of us know, the word 'Trinity' doesn't exist in scripture. It was a pedagogical tool the early Christians used to describe the shape of reality as it was revealed to them. And like many other cultures, they used the geometric symbol of the triad. From the Trimurti of Brahma, Vishnu, and Shiva in the Vedas to the sacred geometry of Pythagoras, from the Trikona in the yantra of Śri Vidya to the Trikaya of Buddhism - the representation of three has the unique capability of representing both the inclusion of opposites, as well as their transcendence. These ideas had an influence on the early Church, and so the dynamic melody of the Trinity has been transposed into new keys over time, and doesn't exactly resemble the Trinity as it first may have been conceived.

The adoption of a literal language around 'Father' and 'Son' as male persons, is partly to blame for that wandering from a coherent pedagogical symbol. This language was issued from the councils of Nicea and Chalcedon as an attempt to stamp out various competing orthodoxies around the shape of the Real, labeled as heresies. One being the Arian, that the person of Jesus was not co-eternal with God. Another was the Monophysite, that Jesus having only one nature was exclusively divine. And the Nestorian: that Christ had two distinct and separate natures, one human and one divine loosely held together. The Church and its bishops attempted to avoid these views by its council determining the fully united, yet somehow different nature of the human and divine, within the person of Jesus as the Christ. Unfortunately, due to the mentioned pressures of the initial counsels in eschewing alternative conceptions, the Christian tradition took this role of the second and third persons historically attributed to the feminine and made it male or neuter in the Son or Spirit. Saint Julian of Norwich rightly sees through this mistake when she reclaims the divine feminine and describes her understanding as:

> "..the property of Fatherhood in Being, of Motherhood in Knowledge, and of Lord-hood in Love, all in one God." [10]

Or even more strikingly in Boehme when he says of the liberated being, "His mother is the Virgin Sophia, the Divine Wisdom, the Mirror of the Being of God." [11]

Of course, although there is no gender in the Godhead, it is the very source and basis of all gender, and as such should be represented in the most accessible way to all that seek it. The complementary use of gendered language in our divine schemas are all simply meant to illustrate the non-duality of two seemingly opposed things, and the brilliant fecundity that follows when their unity is recognized.

But along the way of carving out the retaining walls of proper doctrine, the exclusive humanity of Jesus was overemphasized at the expense of the divine Logos he was *animated by* and was *pointing to*. The etymology of the Latin term *per-sona* (or persons), used to describe the inner workings of the Trinity initially is used to describe an actor's mask, defining the character of their role and *through which* they speak. Sara Grant, of the Society of the Sacred Heart and the Christa Prema Siva Ashram believed this oversight began with the response of the Church to the Arian heresy, the denial of the divinity of Christ.[12] This can be seen in the 'pre-Arian' formulation of the doxology, and the 'post-Arian'.

The current version is:
"Glory be to the Father, and the Son, and the Holy Spirit."

 The initial formula however went like this:
"Glory be to the Father, *through* the Son, *in* the Holy Spirit"

Echoing the passage from Paul in Ephesians, the earlier formulation of the doxologic profession reveals not a static and discrete triad, but a dynamic *perichoresis,* or circle-dance of the infinite. In fear of the divinity of Christ being denied, the Church pushed the pendulum in the other direction, the result of which made him an object to worship or imitate, instead of a reality to *step into.* But this dualistic expression of both the hypostatic union of Christs divine and human natures, and the separate 'personhood' of the Trinity misses the point entirely. The Christic revelation does not divide the transcendant from the immanent, or the human from the divine, but views them from a non-dual whole. As Father Bede Griffiths said, Advaita is *fundamental* to the Christian understanding that we are called to recover: this oneness in the non-dual Being of the Godhead.[13]

THE VIEW FROM WITHOUT

Just like in the first few centuries, there are still many ways to describe this three-fold function of God. From one perspective, there's the 'extrinsic' Trinity: the architecture of God's movement as it appears to us through the stream of time. From another perspective, there's the 'intrinsic' Trinity: the shape of God's own inner life. The 20th century Catholic theologian Karl Rahner called these the Economic and Immanent Trinities. Economic, so called because it is how the immanence of God appears to our limited perspective, and how the efficacy of Her grace is made manifest.

One way to describe the economic aspect is using the formulation from the *sanatana dharma* triad of God, guru, and self. God being God, the guru being the incarnate Logos and God's wisdom within the human form, and self being the same Spirit that is revealed to us as the very vivifying principal of our being.

This Trinity acts as the descent of grace, symbolically and epistemologically reconciling the created order to its proper place in increasing revelation. Where initially God seems a distant Other forever removed from worldly life, we begin to become cognizant of not only the reality of something seemingly 'beyond', but also progressively more confident in our relationship to it. Although we are undoubtedly of a lower status than the Father, we can propitiate and take the position of a trusted servant.

Then that same Father's self-knowing Wisdom and manifestation as Christ comes in the form of the embodied teacher and in the sacred incarnation echoes the words of the Father in Genesis:

It is Good.

For this reason, He is called *Emmanuel* or 'God with us'. The kenotic generosity of God flows forth from alienation to separation, to take on our very limitations in solidarity with us. He tells us the truth about God and about ourselves; of the mistaken ways in which the world seeks esteem, security, and control. He reveals to us how to walk the pathless path, to overcome the world, and to repose in our own innate perfection.

And then he dies.

But instead of getting further away again, returning to the remote recesses of the heavens,

He gets *even closer.*

He goes within us as the experience of Spirit, *Pneuma, Ruach, Prana, Kundalini* that warms the abandoned cavern of the heart and rides like lightning up the spine to the crown of the head bringing us to the reversal and the consummation of this alluring Trinity. We realize either progressively or suddenly, with profound experience or simply a subtle *shift*, our inherent oneness with the Teacher. Knowing that who we really are and who the Guru really is, are *the same who.* That despite the joy we might experience if we have the great privilege of sitting with a living teacher, or from reading their words long after they depart, that we have *never been apart for a single moment*. And even this unitary knowledge mediated in and through the subtle intellect comes to rest in God either before, or after dropping the body.

God moves from beyond us, to beside us, to within us; not just as a precious treasure we hold, but as the center-point around which all our life dances.

THE VIEW FROM WITHIN

Then there's the internal experience of the Trinity. God again is God, and Spirit then takes the second place. Some scholars even say that the Wisdom, Glory, or Sophia of God initially was personified as the Goddess Asherah, the wife of the Semitic God Elohim[14]. The author of John's gospel subsequently recast this role as the Logos for Greek followers who were undoubtedly familiar with the likes of Heraclitus, Parmenides, and Zeno. This role effectively provided the conceptual mechanism necessary for the One to seemingly become many, and was essentially the near-eastern equivalent to Śiva's *Śakti* or power typically personified as a beautiful or terrible Goddess. The third person then is the blissful fruit that proceeds of their union, which composes the entire economic Trinity as the self-communication of God. And as the notable 'Rahner's rule' affirms, these are not two disparate realities separated by space or time, rather that they are mirror images of eachother. The *Radical Trinity* coined by Pannikar additionally lends gravitas to the intuition and mystical knowledge that both the economic and the immanent Trinity are *Advaita*, not two.

Why? Because God *is* Her own self-communication.

So, the Spirit itself is God's action; but this action is not an external movement, but one of unmoving self-recognition or *pratyabhijñana*. This action is itself intrinsic to God's nature and therefore - God doesn't *really* act. Rather, God *is* "pure Act" as Aquinas profoundly state.[15] And all these disparate components of Trinities, since they are nothing aside from the self-reflection of God and therefore not apart from Her, show that the Godhead is that Oneness beneath and through the Trinity, in any formulation.

As Meister Eckhart quips, there is God behind God.

Christ as the eternal Logos from within the body of Jesus passionately advocates for this oneness to be recognized and embodied in each of us in the Gospel of John, saying:

> "And I have given to them the glory you have given me, that they may be one just as we are one: I in them, and you in me, that they might be brought to completion in one, so that the cosmos might know that you sent me forth, and loved them just as you loved me." [16]

Christ in this passage emphasizes *both* the transcendence and immanence of God in an image much like a nesting-doll: Christ, as the unity of the divine and human natures rests in the very center of our being, and at the center of Christ is *God Herself.* This interiorization of increasingly transcendent reality within increasingly immanent experience is meant to both unite and *dissolve* our categories completely. The innermost of our innermost is the paradoxical "*Opposite of opposites... the end without end.*"[17]

Pseudo-Dionysius describes the person of Christ as the reconciling dialectic between the unmanifest and the manifest, in whom all things are held together. Not as the line that divides the water from the Spirit, but as the line that represents their eternal unity. It is likely only due to his anonymity that he escaped the charge of Monophysitism. In other conceptions, like the Spirit-centered theology of William of Saint Thierry, instead of the Son, the Spirit acts as the reconciling third, and is "*not so much to be the spirit proper to each of them (Father and Son) as in fact their communality.*"[18]

Of the more Eastern Orthodox influenced patristics, Saint Gregory Palamas describes it this way:

> "The most sublime Goodness is a holy, awe-inspiring and venerable Trinity flowing forth out of Itself into Itself without change and divinely established in Itself before the ages."[19]

Saint John of the Cross, in the *Living Flame of Love,* describes it in more poetic terms as the hand, the touch, and the burn that are in substance one and the same, only differing in name and form.

> "The first of these gifts is the delicious wound, attributed to the Holy Spirit, and so the soul calls it the "burn." The second is the "taste of everlasting life," attributed to the Son, and the soul calls it the "gentle touch." The third is the "gift" that is the perfect recompense of the soul, attributed to the Father, and is therefore called the "tender hand." Though the three persons of the Most

Holy Trinity are referred to severally because of the operations peculiar to each, the soul is addressing itself to but one essence, saying, "You have changed it into life," for the three persons work together and the whole is attributed to each and to all."

Juan de la Cruz, *The Living Flame of Love*

All of these diverse descriptions, while beautiful and somewhat helpful, continue to remain mostly the purview of academics and theologians. But the vast majority of seekers outside the ivory tower have neither the time, nor the interest to dissect such minutiae. They can offer us a preliminary indirect knowledge, what the Advaitic tradition terms *parokśa jñana*, which can serve to gradually remove unhelpful conceptions of the Divine. And if a seminary education was requisite to participate in the mystery of Spirit, the messenger wouldn't have been a poor carpenter. God is extraordinarily *simple*, and it is that simplicity that is so easily overlooked; it is our minds that are complex. Because the Trinity is not so much an exercise in cosmology,

but in *consciousness*.

This is where I believe other traditions can help us reframe the Trinity in a more transformative or revelatory dimension. Where the Christian Western metaphysic has largely occupied the territory of ontology, the study of what Reality fundamentally is when we view it from the outside, or the wilderness of axiology, the study of meaning or beauty, the great traditions of the East have focused more on the philosophical question of epistemology, the study of knowledge itself. Where the disciplined examination of Being can always be projected outward as if the observing lover of wisdom is peering through a cloudy window onto reality, epistemology avoids this pitfall by observing the process of *perception itself.* Instead of studying the object, divine or otherwise, we study the subject itself. Where in ontology, the Trinity can be seen as a dynamic unitive movement, in epistemology it can be seen as *trans-unitive.* Christ is that transcendent-immanent unification of all dualities; the first and foremost being that of consciousness and being.

The dual function of the Trinity is best described as a movement of Neo-Platonic procession of the macrocosm and return of the microcosm. The procession begins when the one undivided point of dimensionless Being (often termed as the masculine principle), and its eternal Wisdom or Sophia (typically termed as the feminine principle) are timelessly singular with no distance or difference between them. Much like the depiction of Śiva and Śakti in the Tantric traditions, or the yab-yum of Buddhist Tantra, this eternal singleness of the static and dynamic principles is the ground for the manifestation of all experience. We can think of this principle of pure being as pure *sat,* Tillich's *Grund,* Being itself, or even 'beyond being' as we normally know existing things.

Jesus simply called this being-as-such, *Father.*

This reality is not just what 'is', but it is what *shines* with its own aware self-knowledge as *Cit,* or the function of Sophia. In other places, it's termed *Prakasa* and *Vimarśa*: the former being the light of pure knowing, and the latter being the sight of that knowing manifested to itself. In this way, Christ is the eternal self-knowledge God has of Herself. David Bentley Hart in his piercing lucidity beams:

> "Reduced to its most primal origin and ultimate end, then—to what precedes and surpasses the empirical world, what founds and elicits the whole movement of thought in which the phenomenal world subsists— rational life is a finite participation in an infinite act of thought that is also the whole of being: the simplicity of God knowing God."
>
> David Bentley Hart, *You Are Gods*

In the beautifully evocative language of Dzogchen, this is sometimes described as Mother and Child Luminosity – the clarity and self-evidence of being, regardless of its adjuncts. The Bliss or *Ānanda* of this silent oneness is the overflow of joy and fullness or *purnata* that seemingly overflows into the appearance of the world. It is this ecstasy of the One within itself that inexplicably produces a self-forgetting of that essential nature, and subsequently a projecting out of multiplicity. In the magnum opus of Vidyaranya, he comments that this Bliss aspect of Brahman that apparently manifests the world is strangely obscured. Using the illustration of a father listening for the voice of his son in a choir, who cannot isolate the sound of his child due to the admixture of other voices, Vidyaranya says that this Bliss is "known, yet unknown" :

> "Prakriti (primordial substance) is that in which there is the reflection of Brahman, that is pure consciousness and bliss, and is composed of sattva, rajas, and tamas (in a state of homogeneity."
> Panchadasi 1.15

Not only is this blissful effulgence the material cause of the 'descent' into form, but is the irresistible gravity of the Real, endlessly drawing all things to itself.

Even John Ruysbroeck says that:

"..in the hidden depths of our spirit He eternally, ceaselessly, and without intermediary utters a single, fathomless Word, and only that Word. In this word He gives utterance to Himself and all things. This Word, which is none other than, "*See*," is the generation and birth of the Son, the eternal light, in whom all blessedness is seen and known."[20]

When Śakti, the Lords very power as the triad of knowledge, will, and action is metaphorically turned away from Śivas own Self as pure consciousness, the world and its forms are suddenly made manifest. It's this revelation that St. Augustine, channeling Kashmiri Shaivism speaks of in describing humanity as being comprised in miniature of the three faces of the Trinity:

> "The three things are existence, knowledge, and will, for I can say that I am, I know, and I will. I am a being which knows and wills; I know both that I am and that I will; and I will both to be and to know.".[21]

The *jiva* or the isolated being characterized by limited knowledge, limited will, and limited action is in fact an expression of and non-different from the undelimited *Śiva,* the auspicious personification

184

of The Good as such. The return of the limited being to its unlimited origin begins when the animating Śakti or Spirit that composes the essence of the individual metaphorically turns back toward Śiva in an act of *metanoia*, going beyond the rational mind to become one in love. This turning is described as eternally reciprocated by God towards his loyal and his wayward child by Ruysbroeck when he says,

> "The heavenly Father, as a living ground is actively turned toward his Son *as his own eternal wisdom*."[22]

Christ in essence of the modern Trinity takes the place of both roles of power. As Sophia: the eternal knowledge God has of Her own nature; and as Logos: the very Word through which all that is - was made. This Christ truly comprises "*both the Mirror of pure Being, and the Light of a finite world*"[23] as expressed by Evelyn Underhill. She too quotes Ruysbroeck in describing the Word eternally spoken by the Transcendent Silence as being why "*all that lives in the Father unmanifested in the Unity, is also in the Son actively poured forth in manifestation.*"[24]

But Underhill goes on to say that this redemption is not a transactional process of becoming at all, but a *revelation* of the reality of *being*.

185

In Teresa of Avila's seventh mansion of the Interior Castle of the Soul, she describes the three aspects of God being fused into one, where all distinction vanished into a point of simple unity beyond the three centers of divine consciousness called the Trinity. She describes a realization revealing a simultaneity of substance, knowledge, and action, and certainty of the truth that the three are one God. At the height of the two meeting peaks of mystical devotion and divine knowledge, Teresa is found reconciling the two seemingly contradictory metaphysical truths of eternally unfolding Becoming and pure unmoved Being, as the indivisible simplicity of the Absolute, and what Tauler calls the "*end of unity*" in which all diversities sublimate into the rest of their origin and essence.

Where the river of impermanence we are immersed in flows into the Ocean of deathless nectar, of no-birth and no-death, this is that spaceless space where the Son returns to the Father, where Siva and Sakti return to each others loving embrace while truly having never left, where emptiness and fullness lay legs intertwined in indescribable passion. The Vedanta calls this super-essential unity Satchitānanda, or Being, Consciousness, and Bliss. And its visually representative dissolution into the central point, or *bindu* of the Cakra as Brahman – the One without a second.

This sacred geometry of the Yantra makes the Trinity and its function immediately apparent. Instead of a static and two-dimensional triangle, the Śri Cakra displays it as a three-dimensional pyramid connecting emptiness and fullness, formlessness and form in one part-less and indivisible whole. Of course, at the peak of this three-dimensional triad, there is no space, time, or causation. And so, in truth, the action of creation, incarnation, and ascension are all seen as not truly arising as *apart* from that primordial Reality. That the one Godhead is ever the same and is the only reality.

> "To speak of God, however, as infinite consciousness, which is identical to infinite being, is to say that in him the ecstacy of mind is also the perfect satiety of achieved knowledge, of perfect wisdom. God is both the knower and the known, infinite intelligence and infinite intelligibility. This is to say that, in him, rational appetite is perfectly fulfilled, and consciousness perfectly possesses the end it desires. And this, of course, is perfect bliss."

David Bentley Hart, *The Experience of God*

It is here that we see the real import of the fearsome *ajata vada* as described by Śri Guadapadacarya in his gloss on the Mandukya Upanishad. There, the truth of being-awareness, Shiva-Shakti, God-Goddess, Father-Mother, Father-Son, I-Am, are Advaita: not-two. That the Self, the one Reality represented transcendentally and immanently as the Trinity, alone is. The seeming separation of that one Ground on the microcosmic level is individual *avidya,* while the apparently manifold display on the macrocosmic level is the cosmic *māyā.* It may *look like* two in terms of subject and object, or three in terms of the Trinity, or trillions in terms of the world we inhabit. But what it *looks like* and what it *is* are not the same.

We can take this reframing of the Trinity through the lens of its own non-dual heart, and see that the triad of Being, Awareness, and Bliss all correspond to the three 'persons' of God as they seemingly manifest through the medium of time, space, and causation. And without dividing them into separate substances, we can see that being *is* awareness, and awareness *is* bliss. These three descriptors of the Absolute are really one, without a second.

But these are not mere imputations to be grasped conceptually by the intellect. They are meant to be neon signs within the dark night of ignorance, pointing us beyond, or rather beneath the glassy waves of thought, to the vividness glowing within them. We are meant to closely examine, what does this mean for *us?* How do we understand this Reality in relation to our *own* moment-to-moment experience?

How can we go from intellectual knowledge to *experiential truth?*

X

THE MARIGOLD GARLAND

नोदेति नास्तमेत्येषा न वृद्धिं याति न क्षयम्।

स्वयं विभात्यथान्यानि भासयेत् साधनं विना॥५॥

"This Consciousness does neither rise, nor set. It does not increase; nor does it suffer decay. Being self-luminous, it lights up everything else without any help at all."
Drg Drśya Viveka 1.5

The bulk of what has been covered thus far has been primarily to prepare us to walk the pathless path. We have burned away our ignorance and mistaken notions by the fire of practice, and reflected on the truth with the soft glow of the moon-like mind. Now we come to the point at which we allow ourselves to completely disappear into that light of pure knowing like the radiant sun that sits still like a jewel in the sky, illuminating and sustaining all.

JESUS AS FIT TEACHER

In Śankara's classic instructional text, *Vivekachudamani,* or the Crest Jewel of Discrimination, he describes the characteristics of a teacher who has traversed the path to freedom. The qualities that accompany them are:

Srotriya – They are well versed in the scripture and teachings of the tradition. They have the humility to appreciate and imbibe the lived wisdom of those that have come before, knowing that they don't have to re-invent the wheel. They have a deep trust in the validity and efficiency of the tradition to remove obstacles to the innate peace we contain. They are not afraid to employ their own direct experience, but they are not foolish enough to think that they alone have finally "figured it out" for everyone else.

Brahmanishta – They are firmly established in the goal of the teaching, retiring in the lived experience of the Supreme in their daily life. This realization has taken the central place in their life, and everything else has fallen to the periphery.

Karuna – They are an infinite ocean of compassion. Not as a moral value that they acquire or sustain by self-effort, but rather as a natural outflow of the previous qualification. It is because they have turned their back on all that is untrue, that they can turn toward the truth of the world with a wide-open heart – completely fearless. A true teacher always points *away* from themselves, knowing they are but a messenger of a greater unfolding happening on a scale too staggering to perceive. Perhaps this is partly why in the canonical gospels, Jesus' most used epithet to refer to himself is not "Son of God", but *Son of Man.* The teacher truly speaks not from their incarnation, but from *behind it.*

It is here that after all the preliminary aspects of our *sadhana* have corrected our action, purified our heart, and distilled our mind that the fit teacher deems us as *adhikari,* or qualified as a student to be given the highest teaching. We come to realize the deep peace that comes from allowing everything to be naturally as it is, without attempting to change, modify, get rid of, or bypass it, even through spiritual techniques and traditions. Through surrender, forgiveness, and meditation we have trained the mind in calm-abiding. We have become still, and it is this stillness that opens us up to *know.*

> "Be *still* and *know* that I am God! I am exalted among the nations; I am exalted in the earth."
> Psalm 46:10

This is where spiritual ontology, and spiritual epistemology meet. The teacher tells us the truth of what we're experiencing *as we're experiencing it*. In this way, our knowledge and experience come together at first in harmony, and then in simple *unison*.

A WORD ON UNFIT TEACHERS

There is nothing you can offer one who contains everything.

A true teacher will never use sexual power dynamics to sell you freedom, use the guru-student relationship for financial gain, or try to control or micro-manage your life.

They don't flirt with you between sessions or act inappropriately. They don't tune their business model to attempt to maximize the return on investment. They don't try to make you into a carbon copy of their own opinions and habits. They don't care about your gushing endorsement, your evangelical zeal for their personality, vibration, or even teaching. They don't clamor for post engagement and algorithms, elaborate retreat centers or foundations. Truly, you have nothing they want, and that includes money. Why?

"They are fulfilled *in* the Self, *by* the Self."
Bhagavad Gita 2:55

This does not necessarily mean that they teach for free. Only that the sharing of the wisdom that freed them is payment enough. A true teacher, living or not, has only one aim: Your *liberation*.

That is the greatest payment you can give them. *So pay up.* Because whether the teaching principle comes through a living person, scripture, or the wind through the trees, it is each one of us that must take responsibility for our own way of being. The outer form of the teacher is a temporary manifestation, until we realize that the voice has been leading us along the dark passageways of life the entire time has been calling from within the centermost of our own being.

ADHYASA

Like many other oral traditions, Vedanta has a collection of instructive stories, or parables that help to convey the essence of a teaching in a way that is both immediately accessible as well as memorable. One of the most famous of these teaching stories is that of the snake and the rope.

As the story goes, a young man returns to his home after a long day at work. The sun has set, and the shadow of night lays heavily on the land. As he approaches the door to the house, he sees a snake sleepily coiled up along the walkway. Stricken with fear, the boy runs away and stays the night with a friend. The next day, he returns home during the daylight to find the fearsome serpent gone completely. And in it's place lies a single length of heavy and frayed rope – coiled up in just the same way as the sleepy cobra the night before. Upon seeing the truth of the rope, the fear of the snake leaves him immediately and he breaks into a fit of laughter.

Another version, adapted based on Śankara's three-fold definition of suffering goes like this:

A young man returns to his home after a long day at work. The sun has set, and the shadow of night lays heavily on the land. As he approaches the door to the house, he sees a beautiful flower garland coiled up along the walkway. The boy rejoices, thinking about the sweet aroma of the marigolds, the rich color of its bloom, the soft touch of their petals, the taste of the tea made from their blossoms. He runs over and picks up the garland, delighted to show it to everyone he knows.

But upon grasping the floral bouquet, the boy is stung with a blinding pain in the flesh of his arm. He recoils and runs off, for help, the sharp fangs still buried in his limb. The deluge of tears flooding his eyes cloud his vision, and soon he runs smack into the arms of a wandering sage. The wise teacher looks lovingly down at the boy and asks him, "*Why are you afraid?*". The victim explains the saga of the lovely flower garland, and the vicious cobra under its disguise. The old woman looks compassionately on the child and speaks tender words of wisdom.

"What appeared to you in the form of the delightful garland, and what seemed to lash out as the fearsome serpent, are both none other than the harmless bundle of rope you carry under your arm. Here, see." The saint lifts her lantern up high, beaming sheets of light onto the child and his assailant.

The boy glances down at his arm, and immediately the shadow of occlusion, and the fear of projection *vanish*. What coils around his narrow arm is not the sweet garland, nor the ferocious viper, but a harmless length of braided cotton. He rejoices at his original state being restored, and bows in reverence to the teacher.

That in a nutshell is our entire spiritual predicament. Whether it is analogized as a snake and a rope, silver in nacre, a castle in the clouds, the sky in a lake, a city in a mirror, or mirage water in the desert – the takeaway is the same: because of fundamental ignorance (or error in perception) we have superimposed something *unreal* onto the Real, taking the very reality of the Real, and projecting it onto the unreal. This mutual superimposition itself is called *adhyaropa,* or sometimes *anyonya-adhyasa.*

Like a traveler who mistakes the heat from the desert sand for a pool of cool and refreshing water, we mistake the luminous ground of being itself as the divisions of good and evil, past and future, self and other.

In the Synthesis of Yoga, Śri Aurobindo says this:

> "We conceive of ourselves falsely. We see ourselves as we are not; we live in a false relation with our environment, because we know neither the universe nor ourselves for what they really are."

And what are they? Many great souls across time have agreed. Swami Vivekānanda says, "One only exists. It appears as nature, and soul."

Thomas Aquinas puts it even more tersely when he says:

> "God's essence is existence itself."

It is revealed in the very same place where it is hidden. When we look on the world of form, in all its ugliness and heart-breaking beauty, we're truly seeing the manifold nature of the unmodified.

Difference without distinction.

Diversity without division.

Dynamism without demarcation.

When we see duality, what we're really looking at is non-duality, just filtered by the subtle impressions of desire that skew our perception and modify our actions.

But even that error, that *hamartia*, is nothing but the arising of indescribable precision. Before we can speak a word about anything, whether that's a blade of grass or our own awakening, we first make one concession:

It is.

We unnecessarily divide the field of perception, drawing a line down the center of the sand and foolishly claiming there are two beaches. That is until the waves of grace come and wash away all of our foolishness.

The real knowledge of the rope, and the subsequent removal of fear and bestowal of peace, will not be revealed unless the illusory knowledge of the snake falls away. We must remove both our misapprehension of reality, as well as the non-apprehension of reality that is its basis.

We have this persistent misperception because we typically only see the magnificent interior of the castle through the small keyhole we call "I".

The mind, arising as the amalgamation of thoughts, images, sensations, attachments and aversions, and the claiming of them, is the base of all objective knowledge and action. When this mind subsides, as the natural trough to the wave of its arising, the perception of the world does too. Great thinkers before have tried to blaze a solemn trail through the jungle of mind, employing the machete of *neti-neti*, or the via-negativa to cut down all the aspects they can cut down.

But what cannot be negated? What cannot be denied? The French mathematician and philosopher Descartes posited that it is the stream of thought in the individual mind that cannot be denied in his now (in)famous formula: *cogito ergo sum* - "I think, therefore I am.". The literary giant and Oxford don C.S. Lewis in his masterpiece *Mere Christianity* places the God-given faculty of reason in the esteemed place of the undeniable. Vedanta, on the other hand takes both of these functions, classified as *manas,* and *buddhi,* and gives them a penultimate place in the divine hierarchy.

THE MAHAVAKYAS

Atop the epistemological pyramid in the rishi's schema (or the foundation of it, depending on where you're looking from) is not the mind, nor simple reason, but *consciousness itself.* This is the import of the *lakshana mahavakya,* the definition statement - *first of the four* great sayings that distill the conclusion of the Upanishads into their maximum density. The first of these comes from the *Aitereya Upanishad,* found in the *Aranyaka,* or forest literature section of arguably the oldest extant spiritual literature still in existence: the *Rig Veda.* Once the preliminary qualities are developed, the main practice of Vedanta is something reminiscent of Lectio Divina. We begin with *sravanam* (hearing), *mananam* (reflecting), and *nididhyasanam* (meditating). In hearing, we are simply to confirm that we have heard correctly the teaching spoken to us, able to commit it to memory and repeat it back. In reflecting, we are to give full license to our intellect to examine what we've heard, to turn it over and over in our minds, resolving doubts by further consulting the teacher or text. The outcome of these first two aspects is a clarity, and conviction of who we really are. The third step of meditating is to simply stay with and rest in what you've found. This aspect of practice finally brings stability and confidence in your own liberation. Once we know what to look for, and where to look, all that's left is to simply *look.*

LAKṢAṆA VĀKYA

"Prajna-netro loka prajna pratishta *prajñanam Brahma*"

Translation:

> "The Universe has Consciousness as its eye. Consciousness is the basis of all; verily, Consciousness (*Prajñanam*) is Brahman."

It is this first great saying that resounds like a clap of thunder to those with ears to hear. After all, if we are to take Biblical revelation seriously - that God progressively reveals Herself to be nearer and nearer to us as our understanding allows, what could be nearer to us than consciousness *itself?* This is the bold underline beneath the words of the Messiah. That God is not beyond us, nor even just with us, but within us. And as with most of the Upanishads, it is not meant to be blindly swallowed by faith. There must of course be a working trust, pending verification; but there is also a practice implied to allow the truth of the *shruti* to be realized in the sacred ordinariness of our own life. This is the remarkable thing about the meeting point of the devotional love in Christianity, and the transcendent knowledge of Vedanta – both require no esoteric visions, no supernatural insights, no peak experiences, but just the simple nature of our moment-to-moment experience in the world. True spirituality isn't something exotic, foreign, or far-flung from our organic and moment-to-moment experience. In other words, it's completely *ordinary*. It's you, peeling the potatoes, washing the dishes, chopping wood, carrying water.

Not that there's anything inherently wrong with the smells and bells of ritualism, astrological insights, past lives, plant medicine, or the vivid visions of yoginis. But where are they leading you? Are you savoring the nutrients from the meal they prepare? Or are you worshipping the saucepan? There comes a time when these delights may dry up, beckoning us to leave them behind to meet with something still deeper. Unadorned by the extravagance of illumined states, the throws of ecstasy, the heights of altered mind-states, the highest samadhi is the one that is *sahaja*, natural.

Where we remain unfazed by both the mystical, and the mundane as they merge into their source: presence.

The teasing out of this teaching in our direct experience is done most powerfully in the brief text *Drg Drśya Viveka*. Giving as many as six different divisions of meditation, the short treatise gives a lifetime of practical instruction. The most accessible method is typically called the discrimination between the seer, and the seen.

> "Thoughts arising in the mind like desires etc., are the seen. One should meditate on Consciousness as their witness. This is the meditation with duality associated with the seen."
>
> Drg Drśya Viveka 1.24

No discussion of posture, place, or time is discussed in these meditation instructions, because the core principle is itself laid bare. There is no explicit definition between practice on the mat, and practice in daily life because at this point in our path, our whole life as it comes to us is our boundless worship hall. However, whatever it leaves out in minutiae, it makes up for in depth. The import of this verse is that whether on the cushion, or off, whether internally, or externally, the practitioner is to intentionally take the position of the *sakshin,* or the unattached witness of all phenomena.

Essentially the root of the idea as expressed in Drg Drśya Viveka is that any object that can appear to ourselves is not who we are, so the teaching begins with the acknowledgment and negation of what we are not. To find what is true, we begin by removing what is false, like peeling back the layers of an onion.

In the Upanishads this is known as the five sheaths that surround the *sāksin*. We can move through these sheaths from the most gross to the most subtle level.

With each level we can understand that the object of perception is subject to change. The eyes that see are different from what is seen, that much we can instantly confirm with our experience. The seer is one, but the seen are many. And that seeing of the eye itself can be observed by the mind as an object of knowledge. It is subject to change in that we can become blind, or have double vision. We can be aware of our eyes being closed or open, in need of glasses or of light. Now the mind is the knower, and the eye is the known. But from introspection, we can also see that we are aware of the movements of the mind. We can observe our thoughts by placing our attention there, knowing when we are anxious, hopeful, excited, or dejected. This aspect of awareness that is now the witness of the mind shows that awareness and mind are two different things. The light of awareness shines equally on all thoughts, and is single and unchanging.

We are *neti-neti* - not this body, not this mind, not this sensing, perceiving, acting, and not the conscious or unconscious mind. From this we can see that the level of our transient problems and temporary suffering is always at the level of the seen, never of the seer.

After all that isn't essential to our being has been removed, what remains is what we are: the Self or Awareness– the nature of which is *Satchitānanda*.

Infinite *existence*, infinite *consciousness*, infinite *bliss*.

But to make this real to us, the world that appears to us has to be dropped, by the return of the mind to its source. As long as our mind is going out toward the world of objects and forms, we can't see the reality that lies beneath them.   In the Brahma-Jñana-Valimala, Sankara thunders, "*Brahma satyam jagat mithyā*", or the Self is real, and the world is a *lightshow*. The snake, representative of our false ideas of the world appears in the exact same place as the rope, signifying *sat*, or truth. When the mistaken perception of the snake is removed, what remains is the rope. So, when the world is removed, the Self remains.

This may seem intellectual or abstract compared to ordinary meditation. But it is our normal conception of the world that is abstract by comparison. Inquiry is radical simplicity born from natural curiosity. When everything gets dropped, we find this gravity-like pull to become intimately acquainted with what's really going on. It uses the mundane universal experience of simply being as the raw material for our investigation. For practicality, we begin externally with reference to people, places, and things, and *radically disentangle* our identity with them by applying the principle of observation. If we can *see* it, then we cannot *be* it. In other words, if it appears to us within the scope of our perception, it must naturally be *other* than that which perceives.

Internally, we apply the same principle, viewing the *pancakoshas,* or five sheaths, beginning with the physical body itself as an object presented to our consciousness. If I am aware of the body, I cannot *be* the body. After disidentifying with the gross form of the body, we continue to the more subtle aspects like the *prana,* or life-force. This includes the breath, but also all of the internal movements of energy that we experience on a daily basis. Whether we are full of energy, or completely exhausted, it is we who know it. Then deeper still, in the realm of the mind, the seat of our thought flow and emotions, we feel the vacillation of *rāga* (desire), and *dveṣa* (aversion). Even subtler, we come to the intellect, the center of our intuition, or knowing faculty. Whether we know something, or do not know it, both are illumined by something still more encompassing. Beyond the intellect, we may reach a complete blankness of seeming nothingness. This void-like appearance of the complete unknowing of the world is the causal body that stores all the impressions made on our consciousness by our ego-prompted action, and by our reactions to the magic show of the world. This void is at once both an emptiness of all things known, and yet also a fullness of all things in their potential state. But what is it that illumines even this? What is it that is left when we peel away all the layers of the onion? That shining reality is the *Atma*, the Self, and it is not a substance, nor a thing.

It is *you*.

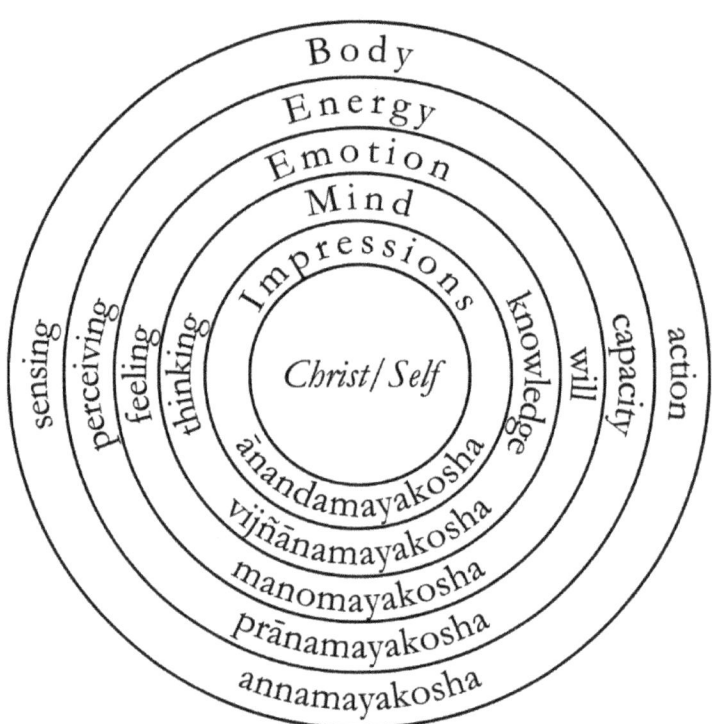

APPEARANCE IS YOUR TRUE BODY

It is important to highlight here that although the preliminary process of Vedantic meditation has us carefully peel away the outer layers of our identity like an onion, this is only part of the process. It is not rejecting the body to withdraw our attachment and identification with it, and it is not a referendum on matter to give Spirit it's proper place. In fact, in the cosmologic system used in this practice, each subtler layer is not apart from the layers above it, but rather *pervades* them completely. Transcendence is not really an upward way, as typically described. It is more accurately an *inward* and a *downward* way. True transcendence *already contains* inclusion, and without it is just an alias for aversion. The world, even your body itself, is not a problem.

Don't get me wrong, identification solely with the vehicle itself is stated in countless scriptures as the *root* of attachment and ignorance. If we're "in here" then everyone else (including God) is: *Out there.*

We're content with the physical body when it brings us pleasure, and discontent when it brings us pain. We pamper it when it brings us joy, and punish it when it brings us misery.

As mentioned in part one, some forms of asceticism call for a mortification of the flesh, as a way of detaching from the pleasure/pain division. But this is often misunderstood and unnecessary. The blows of life itself inflict enough pain already, so we don't typically need to tag in.

Yoga steps in to give us more compassionate practices to follow to purify the body. To render it subtle and responsive, at peace and in resonance with the breath and the mind.

Tantra gives us sadhana to open up subtle channels and nodes of connectivity, loosening knots, to intensify the energy of consciousness in the body. Bringing it up to the crown or out through the eyes.

But the body itself *cannot contain* consciousness. Its walls are far too transient to envelop that which is itself the enveloping of all. True spiritual insight when properly understood, is not a denial of the body, but the *expansion* of it.

All of the kayas, all the tattvas, from the personal God, down to the dust of the earth are only that reflection of the light of Awareness. But this isn't *parinama* (transformation). You don't cease to be what you are in the presence of waking or dream states.

When those states arise, nothing is added. And when they collapse back into consciousness, nothing is lost. This is simply the *vivarana* (appearance) of your true nature, expressed as the bliss aspect of the Godhead.

So, when we truly pay attention to the body we typically identify with, it is seen as an unfindable cloud of sensation and perception, as oscillating luminosity, as *awareness itself*.

So no, your body isn't a problem.

It's just not big enough.

XI

THE GHOST RIVER

"The Self may be compared to the Sun obstructed by dark and dense clouds in sleep, and by light mist in samadhi. For a jñani, the Self shines in its full effulgence like the Sun unobstructed in the heavens."

Tripura Rahasyam 19:115

In *Pancadasi,* the magnum opus of Śri Vidyaranya, he tells a parable to describe the incredible power of the oral lineage tradition to free us from suffering through the simple hearing of the truth.

THE TENTH MAN

In the story there are ten young seekers in search of the hermitage of a revered sage. The eldest of the group was appointed as the leader, entrusted with the safety and guidance of his fellow students.

Their destination lay across a river, benign and shallow, posing no threat to their passage. The group, buoyed by camaraderie and youthful vigor, forded the calm stream to the other shore with no struggle. But having thoroughly searched the village and the forests, the guru was not found.

As they admitted defeat and embarked on their return, the river, swollen by relentless rains, presented a formidable challenge. Its once-placid waters now surged with untamed ferocity. United in purpose yet facing an unforeseen trial, the boys linked arms, attempting to brave the turbulent currents. The river, in its unyielding might, scattered them, each boy tossed helplessly downstream.

Miraculously, all were cast upon the opposite bank, disheveled and drenched, but alive. The leader, with a sense of grave responsibility, lined up his companions to account for each one. He counted: one through nine, his heart sinking with each number. The realization was swift and dreadful – one among them was missing, presumably claimed by the river's wrath.

Recounts ensued, each tally ending at nine, each count deepening their despair. Mourning for their lost brother, they were engulfed in grief, the leader most of all, burdened by the weight of responsibility and perceived failure.

Unknown to the boys, the precious teacher had observed this entire episode from a distance. With a mixture of amusement and empathy, he approached his distraught disciples, disguised as a simple beggar. Listening to their tale of loss, he offered to count them himself. As he counted each boy, he reached nine and then, turning to the leader, he declared with a gentle smile, "And *you* are the tenth."

In that moment, a profound realization and deep gratitude dawned upon each one of the boys, particularly the eldest. The tenth boy was in fact never truly lost; his presence throughout the ordeal was constant, only overlooked in the chaos and fear. Their previous sorrow transformed into relief and understanding.

UPADEŚA VĀKYA

Once the *parokṣa jñana,* or indirect knowledge of reality is tasted, it must then be broken down for digestion. It must be gnawed upon, masticated, turned over and over in the mouth of the mind until no doubt is left behind. Only then can it be swallowed and assimilated into our being, transforming the bread into the body in the innermost act of communion. The second sequence of teaching comes from the Chandogya Upanishad of the Sama Veda. In the text it builds and expands upon the first pointing-out instruction of "Brahman is Consciousness." to answer the student's natural progression of inquiry. If the 'God beyond God' that Meister Eckhart describes is nothing but pure consciousness, then where *is* that consciousness?

> "As, dear boy, the bees make honey by collecting juices from different trees and reduce them into one essence, and there, as these juices have no such discrimination as 'I am the juice of this tree, I am the juice of that tree'; even so, dear boy, all these creatures having merged into Being, do not know, 'We have merged into Being.' Whatever these creatures are here, tiger or lion or wolf or boar or worm or flying insect or gadfly or mosquito, that they become again. That Being which is this subtle essence, even That all this world has for itself. That is the true. That is the Atman. *That thou art, O Svetaketu.*"
> Chandogya Upanishad 6.9.1-3

After the learned student Svetaketu returns home from his studies and thinks himself accomplished, his father Uddalaka sees his conceit and playfully asks him, 'If you know so much, did you learn that by knowing which, all else is known?'. To his surprise, the boy had not been given this secret of secrets, and so the sage carefully explains to him that the real knowledge isn't found somewhere in books, nor in the mountain caves, but within himself. The pure consciousness which was described as the Absolute Godhead in the first great saying is further pointed out as not 'out there' somewhere in space, or to be attained at a later time, but in the deepest *here* and the closest *now*. It is to be intimately known as our very *Self*, unmediated by any descriptive attribute. The statement '*Tat Tvam Asi*' or That Thou Art comprises the *upadeśa mahavakya,* or the teaching statement – designed to take us from merely conceptual knowledge to unmediated knowledge. We solidify that priceless gift from the teacher of the glimpse of unmediated knowledge by investigating immediately into the nature of our own tenth person; by inquiry into our very identity.

YOU'RE IT

Self-Inquiry is a teaching popularized by Śri Ramana Maharshi, a Tamil saint from the early 20th century. Based on the ancient Vedic practice of *atma-vichara*, self-inquiry is the quintessential practice for those on the path of knowledge, and is sometimes called the Maha or Great Yoga. *Vicharasangraham* and *Nan Yar* were the first printed set of instructions for the practice in Ramana's own words. In them, he describes the direct path of self-realization or liberation through the path of Jñana yoga. The themes of non-attachment, wisdom, and dedication are prevalent throughout, and described as essential components of attaining the quiescence of mind required for inquiry.

Although Śri Ramana was described as a proponent of the path of jñana yoga or the path of union through knowledge, he did not discourage other forms of spiritual practice such as karma yoga or service, and bhakti yoga – the devotion to God or Goddess. But ultimately, self-inquiry has more in common with jñana yoga in that it is a practice of *experience*, investigating realities that are common to all.

The main practice of self-inquiry is to pose the question to yourself, "who am I?" which arguably sounds too simple to actually be good for anything. However, to hear the answer to this question, the mind must become resolutely quiet.

But unlike the traditional Vedantic method, the self-inquiry posed by Ramana is not so much a negative approach, but a positive one.

When the mind that is subtle goes out through the brain and the sense-organs, the gross names and forms appear; when it stays in the heart, the names and forms disappear. Not letting the mind go out, but retaining it in the Heart is what is called "inwardness". So when the mind stays in the Heart, the 'I' which is the source of all thoughts will go, and the Self which always is will shine. Think of it like this:

A shard of a mirror is lying on the ground in an open field in full sunshine. The light that falls on that glass is reflected and strikes the wall in a dark room, illuminating the objects inside. The reflected light when seen on the wall, is in the same shape as the piece of mirror, but the direct sunlight that illuminates the mirror itself shines in all directions. The Existence-Consciousness of the Self is like the sunshine, and the ego is like the reflected ray stretching from the mirror to the wall of the room. Just as the reflected ray takes on the limitations of the size and shape of the mirror, the ego feeling experiences the size and form of the body and takes it to be "I".

Self-inquiry is the act of the person, after growing disinterested with the objects in the room, longing to find the source of the illumination. To find the source, we simply have to go to the spot where the light strikes, then turn around, tracing the beam back.

Once the shard of mirror is reached, that is the point of the mind dissolving in the heart. The length of the reflected ray reduced to zero, where no illumination of objects is possible, this is perceived by many as the maha-sunya or great void of ego dissolution. Because we might be blinded at first, having been within a dark room, but now we stand in the open field itself, where the light of the sun shines infinitely brighter.

This is the realization that the mirror itself was never the *source* of the light, but simply a reflector.

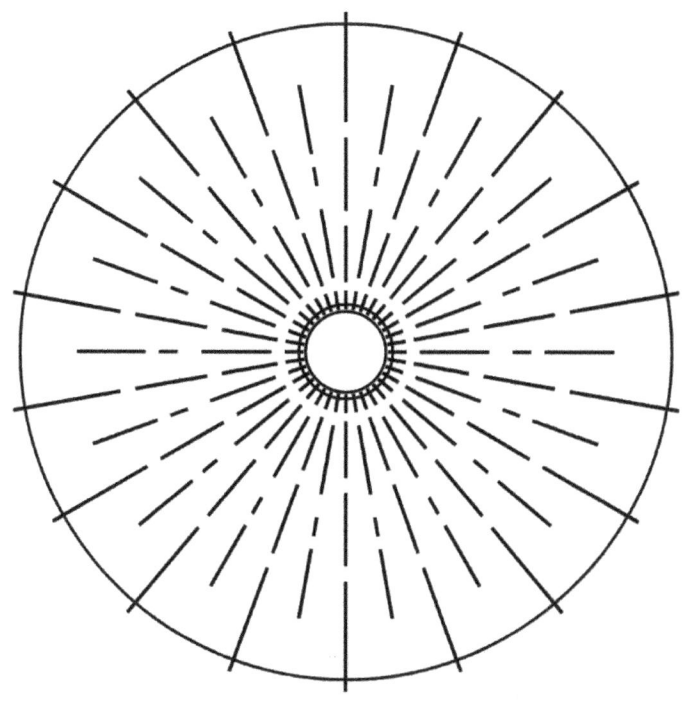

According to Vedanta, the world only appears because our limited sense of "I" (the mirror) appears first in the space of the heart as the mind's origin. Śri Ramana says:

> "Of all the thoughts that arise in the mind, the 'I' thought is the first. It is only after the rise of this that the other thoughts arise. It is after the appearance of the first personal pronoun that the second and third personal pronouns appear."

In other words, without the *ahamkara*, literally the 'I-thought', there is no You-thought, or Them-thought. Without the First person, there is no second or third.

To quiet the mind, we must go directly to this sense of I by inquiring 'Who am I?'. The object isn't to get an answer to the question in the form of another thought, but to feel that self-illuminating awareness that is the ground of all being. The thought 'who am I?' will dissolve all other thoughts, including the "I" thought, and like the stick used for stirring the burning pyre, it will itself in the end get destroyed. Then, reality stands revealed as it ever was. In this way, it isn't necessary to scrutinize every thought, but to scrutinize *who* those thoughts appear to. Because this I-thought has a property where when we intensely investigate it, it dissolves on its own. The tenth man is really the only man, representative of pure awareness unmodified and unmixed with what appears to it. The ego itself acts as a false first person, and when the light of attention turns back on it, it disappears as nonexistent. The inquirer then has nothing more to do, and is established in and *as* the Self.

This is not a finite self with an individual history, that is or has a body or mind or soul, that is moved by wants and needs and hopes and dreams. The Self is that untouched Being which first spoke to Moses in the desert; that which is self-shining within the secret cave of the heart as the stainless knowledge:

"I am that I am."

Tat tvam asi.

The method goes like this:

Find a place to sit where you won't be disturbed and can give the inquiry your full attention.

Keep your eyes open, and take a few deep breaths, allowing thoughts and objects of perception to fade away into the background of awareness.

Now gently and with an open-handed curiosity, ask yourself the question: Who am I?

At first, conditioned responses might arise like the thought of your name, or the thought of your body, or your relationships, or your memories or life events.

But recognize these as not essential to you, but just thoughts appearing to you.

When thoughts arise, don't pursue them but simply ask: 'To whom does this thought appear?'

It doesn't matter how many thoughts arise.

As each thought comes up, respond with "to who?"

The answer that would come would be "to me".

Then inquire again "Who am I?"

Don't focus on an answer to the words as "I am", but the inner feeling of it, without needing the addition of words.

Go directly to your own beingness.

Then the mind will go back to its source; and the thought that arose will subside.

Abide as yourself in that sense of 'I' for a while.

With repeated practice in this way, the mind develops the power to stay in its source.

Once in that source, the attention loses its propensity to stretch out, and the curtain falls away to reveal the unrobed lacuna of ourselves.

But who does this void appear to?

XII

LIKE GOLD

न तत्र सूर्यो भाति न चन्द्रतारकं नेमा विद्युतो भान्ति
कुतोऽयमग्निः। तमेव भान्तमनुभाति सर्वं तस्य भासा सर्वमिदं
विभाति॥ १४॥

na tatra sūryo bhāti na candra-tārakam nemā vidyuto bhānti
kuto'yam-agnih, tameva bhāntam-anubhāti sarvam tasya bhāsā
sarvam-idam vibhāti

"The sun does not shine there, nor does the moon, nor the stars. The
lightning does not shine there, much less this fire. When He shines,
everything shines after Him. By His light alone do all these shine."
Mundaka Upanishad 2.2.10

T he third of the mahavakyas comes from the shortest of all the principal Upanishads, and arguably the most powerful of them. It is frequently said in some schools of Vedanta that we can get the entire truth from the Mandukya

229

with the gloss of Gaudapada and the commentary of Śankara. If one doesn't fully understand the import of that, then they can open their study to the rest of the principal and minor Upanishads.

ANUBHAVA VĀKYA

After negating all that appears to us as an object of consciousness by discernment and dispassion, untangling pure consciousness from the world we typically take as self-existing – we have reached the pinnacle of the ancient Sankhya philosophy of Kapila. This is where many seekers unfortunately think that Vedanta takes them, but it is simply a pedagogical step in the process of inquiry. There are many differences between the two systems, including the multiplicity of consciousnesses, and the eternally separate nature of matter posited by the Sankhyans. Vedanta stands apart in these two specific areas due to its insistence on the *oneness* of consciousness – both with itself, and its appearance. This is the import of the *anubhava vakya*, the statement on the point of experience.

Using the primordial seed mantra of 'Om' that served as the book-ends for every Vedic ritual enacted by the rishis, the character is invoked from the beginning of the Upanishad as both the symbol and the referent of the one indivisible reality of Brahman. The division of Om into parts, just like the division of the Absolute into parts, is simply for the sake of instruction and is in no way definitive. Advaita consistently points to Reality as *niśkalam*, or partless; Śankarācārya himself asserts that it is only the fourth in the series of discussion. This separation of the states of consciousness represented by Om is an entire path of study and outside the scope of this book. However, the great-saying in the second verse can be taken up for our purposes.

> "All this is verily Brahman. This Ātman is Brahman. This
> Ātman has four quarters (parts)."
> Mandukya Upanishad 1.2

Ignoring the previously mentioned reference to the *catushpada*, or four parts, the mantra fires off two cannon-blasts from its pages. The first *sarvam hyetad*, or 'All this', describes anything at all that can be designated as 'this' or 'not I'. It is here that we regain all that we previously sieved out in our via-negativa. Whatever we disidentified with as external and non-essential to our natural being is reclaimed from the perspective of pure awareness. This is the implicit 'tantric' aspect inherent in Vedanta that complements the path inward with the balancing of the path outward. But if we were just going to rejoin with all we previously cut away, why wouldn't the wisdom of the teachers allow us to just merge with the world from the beginning?

Because we cannot become everything without first becoming *nothing*.

We need both parts of the path. The intimate tantric interconnection with the world around us leading to the pleroma of bliss, as well as the śūnyatā or complete emptiness of self and form that all things arise from. We tend to believe the hype of the mindfulness industry that it's about self-improvement instead of self-relinquishment. Or that it's all about abstract philosophy, or all about silent meditation. Or that we can have our cake, and eat it too. Then we just get caught on the snares of the world, the *anitya* or impermanence of Buddhism. This is again what Jesus was referring to when he warned against building our house on sand. When we place our identity in anything that is subject to change, we're bound to feel threatened by the loss of that thing. When we try to "be one with everything" as a separate person, we may only get as far as a conceptual understanding of the physiological unity of life, or an intellectual understanding of the transcendent unity of pure being. But there's much more than that.

Oneness cannot be simply understood with the mind, but must be felt vibrationally with the heart, and lived causally by the spirit. But to ascertain this, the walls that we put up to divide "I" from everything else, need to come tumbling down. And when they do, we realize that as Nisargadatta Maharaj said, we are both everything, *and* no-thing.

Because really, unless a grain of wheat falls to the ground and dies, it won't produce any fruit.

The second sentence in the mantra states that it is this very Self that is the attributeless Godhead, the 'one, without a second'. The difference between the import of this point and the first and second mahavakyas is that now this Self is regarded not as something separate from the play of universal appearance, but as one seamless identity with it.

THE ROOM

There was a woman standing in the dimly lit corner where two walls meet. She had been standing there for as long as she could remember; almost as if she was born in that dark room. Over time she began to feel like she didn't belong there, like she needed to get out. She started to grope blindly along the walls with both hands and crying, "How can I be free of this triangular room?" A friend standing at a distance heard her crying and turned to speak to her.

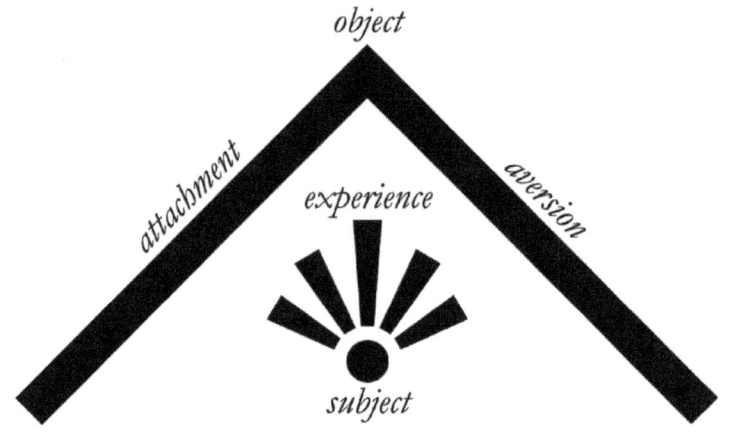

There were only two walls in that open space, both meeting together at the ends. The friend realized that the woman had uncritically assumed that the room had three walls, but never actually turned around to check. So, she asked her, "Try searching for a way out on the third wall behind you!". The woman turned around and realized that there was no obstacle, and being relieved, runs in that direction. The friend asks her, "Why are you running?

If you walk slowly, will you remain imprisoned?"

metanoia

We cannot grok the nature of reality from the perspective of the third person, nor the second. It is only in the ground of the first-person that the second and third glitter in response. This is truly the metanoia that Jesus spoke of in his first message to the poor fishermen of Galilea. Unfortunately, the Latin fathers of the early centuries decided to translate the one word that encapsulates the core of Jesus' teaching as *paenitentia* or penance – indicating an assumption of guilt and repentance. Most modern scholars however, define metanoia as a change of heart, a going beyond (meta) the mind (noia). This about-face, this turning around of the heart-mind from the two walls of duality that appear to have us bound is the true metanoia. It is the thinking again, or thinking twice about our current situation that results in the re-cognition of our inherent freedom.

Here we forever snap the knot of the heart we were tied into. Knowing that our ego (the limited notion of identity with one portion of reality to the exclusion of another) was never truly real, that we were never bound and were never freed, but always exist and shine as the referent of *I am*.

No imprisonment, no release.

This is what Gaudapada trumpets in his karika when he says that the *turiya*, the silent 'fourth' aspect of Om is in fact the entire reality of the three previous divisions. When we wake up in a sweat in the middle of the night, seeing out of the corner of our eye a terrifying shadowy figure standing ominously in the corner of our bedroom, what we're really looking at is the dim and blurry form of the jacket hanging on our door, we just see it incorrectly. When we see duality, what we're really 'looking at' is non-duality, we're just perceiving it incorrectly. But even that incorrectness of perception is *also* non-duality. The illusion appears in the *exact same place* as the truth does. *Don't look elsewhere.*

To make real the truth indicated in this third mahavakya, we can undergo the practice of *vyapti*, or sublimation. Essentially, this technical term refers to mutual concomitance, or the relationless relationship between two things. The Vedanta calls it *aspar's'a* yoga, what my teacher defined as the touch of the untouched. The typical example used for this is that of smoke and fire. Although there can sometimes be cleanly burning fire without the effect of smoke, if smoke is present, fire itself is present as the very substantive cause of it. This is the very last of 15 exhaustive elucidations of non-dual meditation given by Sri Sankaracarya in the practical handbook *Aparokshanubhuti*.

> "Having reduced the visible to the invisible, the wise should think of the universe as one with Brahman. Thus alone will they abide in eternal felicity with the mind full of consciousness and bliss."
> Aparokshanubhuti 142

After having seen the face of emptiness directly by way of hearing the words of the teacher, assimilating them in the understanding, and resting in their inner meaning, we have open access to return to that experiential knowledge through whatever means, or no means at all. But as the world of appearances still rumbles on, this embodied practice of sublimation offers us an incredible entry point to the Spirit hidden as all form. Initially, the objects of our perception, and the identification of ourselves as the perceiver, can seem like obstacles to enlightenment. The split between subject and object that carries with it all the superficial joy and suffering of the world. Over and over we're told that true freedom is our deepest essence, but then what obstacle could there possibly be to who we really are?

When awareness, of its own free nature apparently diffracts into the triad of knower, known, and knowledge - all of existence is known as your own activity. All that appears to you is not a limitation, but what Śri Kśemaraja calls the *glimmering* of your own nature.

Taken up later by modern wisdom teachers like Sri Atmananda Krishnamenon, Rupert Spira, Francis Lucille, and Greg Goode, this phenomenological approach bridges the seemingly disparate modalities of Advaita Vedanta and Śaiva or Śakta Tantra into a non-dual unity.

We begin by taking something visible, or perceivable in some way. Something we typically describe as being 'outside of us' as an object present to our sense faculties. The object could be an apple, a candle, or anything stationary and not covered with text. Right now, look up and out into your immediate environment. Select something unmoving to place your attention on, whether it's a computer monitor, a couch cushion, anything. Dropping any conceptual elaboration in reference to the object, just notice what is immediately present within your own intimate experience of it. If you had no recollection or discursive knowledge of this particular object, what could you say about it? If you are a person with average vision, you might discern the elements of tone or *hue*, and of shape, or *pattern*. These aspects both visually represent to us the form of the object. Look and see for yourself that right at the very edges of the thing you're focusing on, if you rely simply on your visual faculty rather than memory, the only difference between the object and the surface it rests on is a variation of color and difference in shape. Even distance and texture are just modulations of those same two characteristics.

Now what is the ground, the substratum of this appearance? What is it that without which, neither form nor the color and shape that constitute it can be found? Both of them can really be boiled down to the raw experience of *seeing*. You really cannot separate out the form from the basic seeing of it. So, we never truly see 'form' per se, but rather we see the seeing itself.

Continuing on, what is there to this seeing other than the simple knowing that illumines it? Keep your attention trained on the appearance and genuinely inquire – can I separate seeing from knowing? You'll no doubt find that you cannot, because there really aren't two things, seeing and knowing existing as separate aspects. And this knowing principle, what are its defining characteristics? Does it have form, color, shape, texture?

Now close your eyes. There may be difference introduced in the presence or absence of the lower characteristics of form. You may be able to say the appearance that was present a moment ago is not present in current experience. But what is that on which the knowing or the not-knowing depends? Here you may be at a loss for words, not being able to determine a name for the intimacy of this direct experience. But for ease of further conversation, we can simply say: *Awareness*.

The object 'out there' is nothing *other* than the form presented to us, and the form presented to us is nothing *other* than the seeing of it. The seeing of it is nothing *other* than the knowing of it, and the knowing of it is nothing *other* than awareness itself. They cannot be shown separately, and so are established in direct experience as non-dual, not two. This is the practical and accessible method expressed in *Aparokshanubhuti* of dissolving the visible effect into the invisible cause, recognizing each layer of experience to be completely pervaded (*vyapti*) by the one beneath it. And we can practice this on all of our sense faculties, not just vision. Tasting, touching, smelling, and hearing can and should also be taken up for examination, to dissolve the solidity and separateness of our own revolving doors of the in/finite. Each faculty is like the diffraction of the light rays of a self-illuminating prism. Through the power of consciousness to apparently localize itself as a finite mind, it beautifully splays into the spectrum of ROYGBIV, distributing the creative vibrancy of its own light. Even the disparate waves of visual frequency are never at any time *other* than the ecstatic excitation of that pure light.

The material and efficient cause of the world is the purity of the limitless light of knowing. And it is the infinity of that knowing that gives it the lustre of self-knowledge. That endless 'I' makes up all the folds of space and time, and gravity is the shimmer of its love for itself.

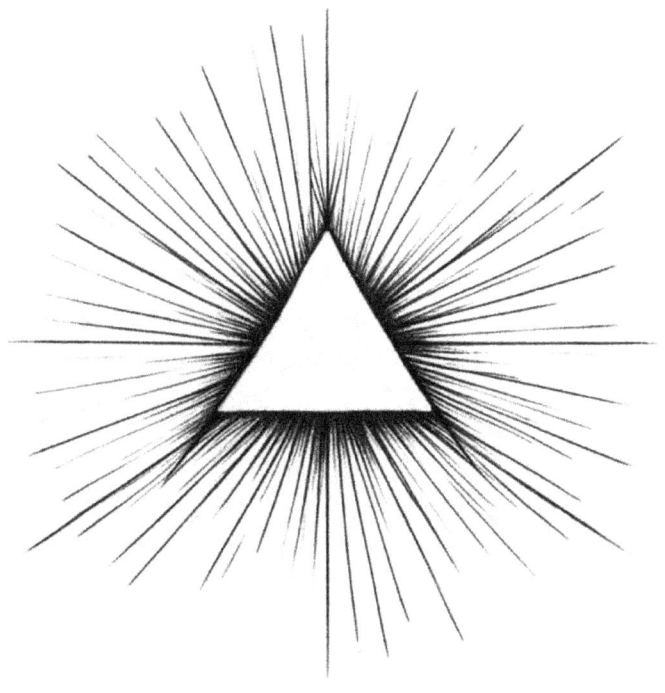

This is the deeper meaning behind the symbolism of traditional Hindu ritual worship. Elements are offered to the deity as the personification of Absolute Awareness – the butter lamp for seeing, the bell for hearing, the sandalwood for smelling, the flowers for touching, and the water for tasting.

In this symbolic worship, all of our sense faculties and the objects they contain are sublimated within the all-encompassing embrace of the God beyond God:

Awareness.

Go directly to that unfindable knowing that is the empty luminosity of awareness itself. Look directly at it. Really stare it down.

Center right in on it for a minute or so, but relax — loosen up just a little bit. Get comfortable in it.

Once you have a feel for that, allow that very same awareness to rest in the open space out in front of you. Stay with that for a moment or so, then center right back in on awareness. Go back and forth like this for just a little while.

Now allowing these to blend completely together, come to rest gently in the center. The self-revealing nature of awareness is simultaneously still and yet playfully arises as the entire visual field.

All sensations and perceptions reflect as the manifest form of aware being, without exception. When a movement of mind arises, unflinchingly see that it does not arise, remain, or depart.

There has never for a moment ever been a second reality other than this pristine space of presence.

Unbounded perfection in all directions, end without end.

And that's all there is to it.

XIII

NOTHING LEFT OUT

"All those men who are raised up above their created being into a contemplative life are one with this divine brightness and are that brightness itself. And they see, feel, and find, even by means of this Divine Light, that as regards their uncreated nature, they are that same simple ground from which the brightness without limit shines forth in a godlike manner, and which according to the simplicity of the essence remains in everlasting, modeless simplicity."

Jan Van Ruuysbroeck

T he wise say that if we know how to look deeply enough, every bush burns. But it is not because there exist countless small fires igniting across the countryside. We need not transform the world, but simply our own way of being and seeing. This is how Jesus takes the revelation of Moses on Mount Horeb and transposes it to a higher octave. "Jesus not only has a relationship with the radiance, with the burning, but Jesus himself becomes it." 25

246

"And after six days Jesus takes Peter, and James, and his brother John, and privately leads them up to a high mountain. And he was transfigured before them, and his face shone out like the sun, and his garments became as white as light."

Matthew 17:1

THE PRINCESS OF KASHI

The story goes that there was a Prince of a vast kingdom in ancient India where in the royal court a play was arranged. And in the drama, one of the characters was to play the role of the little girl who was the beloved of her own vast kingdom, the Princess of Kashi.

The royal administrators couldn't find a little girl of the right age and temperament to play the role, so the Queen requested that the young Prince be dressed up to suit the role. As the Prince was a little boy at that time, around four or five years old, he was easily fit into an elaborate silk sari, decked in gold, and beautifully jeweled plaits in his hair to play the part of the Princess.

The play was staged, and the Queen was so delighted with the Prince's appearance that she asked the court painter to make a portrait of the boy. He titled it the Princess of Kashi, dated it and framed it up.

15 *long* years passed.

The prince was quite grown up, 20 years old now. After his mother's death, he was now charged with attending to the affairs of the Kingdom with skill and compassion. One day he was searching the palace library for a document, and he wanders off into one of the old storage rooms underground. As he surveys the space, he examines the old trinkets and artifacts and his eyes come to rest on this old painting. He moves closer and wipes the dust off of the gilded frame, and sees the inscription - Princess of Kashi. He says to himself:

"Look at the date, she must be near the same age as me!"

He takes the painting back up to his chambers personally and hangs it on the wall, staring at it day after day. Wondering, where could this Princess be now? How do I find her? He begins to fall in love with her and makes the firm resolve:

"This is the Princess I want to marry. Until I find her, I don't think I'll ever have true happiness."

The royal attendants begin to notice something off with the Prince's behavior. He stays mostly in his room, mopes about from time to time, and doesn't seem to be interested in his previous endeavors anymore.

Finally, a wise minister goes and asks him, "What ails you Prince? You can confide in me."

The Prince looks expectantly at the minister and says, "Well what can I tell you? I am in love."

"Very good! Who is she?"

"She's the Princess of Kashi."

"Good, a Princess! Where did you meet her?"

"I haven't actually met her, but I've seen her portrait. I'll show you, it's a beautiful old painting. It was painted when she was a young girl, the date says 15 years ago. I've searched the court records, all the scrolls and books, and I can't find anything written about her anywhere. Maybe you could help me?"

The minister is curious, and so follows the Prince to his chambers to lay eyes upon this famed portrait. As they arrive, it begins to dawn on him. The minister pauses, recalling the events of the stage play so many years ago. He then tells the Prince to sit down.

"That is not the Princess of Kashi."

"Whoever she is I'll marry her" The Prince says.

"No Prince, you do not understand. You see, many years ago there was a drama staged in the court for the Kings pleasure, and it was required for the cast to have a person who would play the part of the young Princess of Kashi. After a search, *you* were found to be suited perfectly for the role. There is no Princess of Kashi. Through misperception and imagination, you have fallen in love with *yourself*, dear Prince."

As the story illustrates, the *sankalpa* or desire in the form of "I want this" began to swell from the moment that the Prince superimposed his own happiness and completion onto an external figure. And that same desire altogether disappeared from his mind at the very moment that the knowledge dawned of her non-existence as anything *other* than his very own creativity. He could not fulfill the desire externally, because the Princess of Kashi does not exist apart from him. But that desire rather than being fulfilled, comes to rest in its own source of fulfillment. He alone is the Princess of Kashi and always has been. When one realizes the truth about oneself and that the Princess of Kashi is none other than me, then the mind does not form limiting desire because there is no *separate reality* to grasp. And when the limiting desire evaporates in its place, attachment and aversion go with it. This non-grasping, ever free mind is no mind, and this is freedom.

This is what primarily differentiates the path of yoga, and the pathless path of non-duality. The Prince here never truly shuts his eyes, does not occlude his sense faculties, does not bother to stop the mind. Here the yogic path may have said, "Don't look at the Princess of Kashi, keep your eyes closed! If you keep your mind constantly in an absorbed state, you will then be free". Although this expression of practice is extremely helpful in bringing stillness to the mind that is typically required for clarity to dawn, the non-dual path offers a more direct route to not just apprehending this truth on a discursive level, nor of simply glimpsing it, but of stabilizing the recognition in equanimous perfection. Contrary to this parable, the reality to which the metaphorical portrait of the prince refers is not truly a second thing apart from his own being. Rather, the unfurling of the painting of the universe is done on the canvas of Consciousness itself. [26]

ANUSANDHĀNA VĀKYA

The last of the great sayings comes from the Brihadāranyaka Upanishad of the Yajur Veda. It comes after the evocation statement, the teaching instruction, the experiential expression, to bring us to the *anusandhāna vākya,* or the point of confidence. This statement epitomizes the nearest phonetic expression of the truth realized within the subtle intellect that:

o Our essential identity is *not* exclusively associated with the 'outer' world, the physical body, or the mind.

o What or Who we really are is *avyopadeśa* - absolutely indescribable by the lexicon of the finite mind.

o All that appears to us is in fact none other than our *inherent* capacity of self-expression within the domain of self-reflectivity.

Wisdom once again peals:

"This self was indeed Brahman in the beginning. It knew only Itself as, 'I am Brahman'. Therefore, It became all." Brihadāranyaka Upanishad

Whereas most of Vedanta is pedagogical in nature, mostly centering its discourse on explicitly pointing to the truth and how to recognize it, there is a less emphasized and more implicit treatment of the remaining phenomena that continue to appear to us. The Śakta oriented tantra traditions in contrast spend more time explicitly naming this consummation of the spiritual path as *purnahamta*, the fullness of 'I'. To the everyday mind, the world happens *at* us and *to* us. To the awake, the world happens *in* us and *through* us. This non-dual swallowing of dualism is also present within the heart of the Christian tradition.

> *"There is light within a person of light, and they light up the whole world."*
>
> Gospel of Thomas, Logion 24

This is however, not just a solipsistic affair, or the scholastic boogeyman of an imagined 'gnosticism'. Panikkar again elucidates this spectrum of relation of the Platonic One and the many as a complete yet unending continuum of knowing.

"These yous manifest an ontological gradation that ranges from a pure consciousness of the trinitarian thou to our empirical consciousness of material things."[27]

Indeed, as Hart confirms, every finite 'I' is simply a "created inflection of God's eternal 'I AM' in the mystery of the Trinity"[28]. One of the simplest ways to illustrate this truth on the microcosmic level is via the example of the dream state. When we fall asleep at night, we pass over the twilight stage of the hypnogog, and the darkness of self-forgetfulness ensues. Once thoroughly shrouded in blankness, the creative power of our own mind manifests the dream body, the dream world, and the various objects and entities that inhabit it.

Imagine you are a waitress at a restaurant in your hometown of Boise, Idaho. After a long day waiting tables, you crash on your sofa and drift off. After a timeless period of what seems like nothing at all, you find yourself thrown into another world. But because this particular movie lacked the opening credits, it seemed as if it was just a continuation of your normal life, yet somehow different. You began your morning commute to the financial district of New York City for a blistering day of managing commodity futures. Your first few moves seem to be flawless. Despite having next to zero knowledge of economics, you adeptly navigate the market to the acclaim of your team and shareholders. But toward the afternoon, you start to slip. You begin making bad deals, ones that dig at your coffers and threaten to leave you destitute and penniless. Just as you're about to be angrily thrown out into the street, you wake up on your twin mattress in Boise drenched in anxiety, but relieved. At any point of the dream if you were to come to lucidity, you would recognize that you are not in fact the financial savant walking the bustling streets of New York or any city for that matter, but are warm in your midwestern coverlet. In truth, not just are you *not* what you appear to be in the dream, but the dream itself (including the vast city and its goings on) is nothing other than the very radiance of your own being. In this way, the awakening process is more like coming into a clear wakefulness as in a lucid dream. The dream objects and circumstances still appear to us, but they are recognized for what they are: not a *second* reality apart from the dreamer themself.

You are the dimensionless mirror of aware being. Everything you see, hear, taste, touch, smell, emote, or think—every image reflected in the mirror of the Self may look like *idam*, this, but in truth is simply 'I'. Not as a finite subject, but that blazing wholeness to which 'I' refers. Completion is not found in simply the negation of the limited 'I', but in the *recognition of its referent*.

> "That awareness is the Self of the universe, which is able to manifest both itself and that which is apparently other. It is explained to be a unitary 'I.'"

255

The counterpart in linguistic mysticism that drives this point home for tantrikas like Abhinavagupta and Kśemaraja is the constant reminder that both the first letter in the Sanskrit alphabet: *A*, and the last letter: *ha*, united in their convergence as: *m* – comprise the entirety of their sacred semantic structure, a holographic representative of the macrocosm. This marriage of these letters in the language of the ancient seers of the Vedas results in the highest and most secret of all mantras: *Aham*.

I.

XIV

IT IS FINISHED.

यस्त्वात्मरतिरेव स्यादात्मतृप्तश्च मानवः।
आत्मन्येव च सन्तुष्टस्तस्य कार्यं न विद्यते॥ १७॥

yastvātmaratireva syādātmatrptaśca mānavah, ātmanyeva ca
santustastasya kāryam na vidyate

*"But the person who rejoices only in the Self, who is satisfied with the Self,
who is content in the Self alone, for Them verily there is nothing more to be
done."*

Song of the Lord 3:17

he **T**supreme goal in life, at least from the pinnacle
perspective of the great unified tradition that all
religions and spiritual paths belong to, is giving
up the age-old struggle against the relentless current of the
universe. Whether it's the Greek Orthodox Church and its
description of divine *theosis,* or deification; or in the blown-out

flame of *nirvana* – the names and forms of practice, in addition to the words and images used to describe that reality once the conceptual mind returns are conditioned by the temporal, spatial, and cultural factors surrounding that revelation. The pure content of the revelation itself, however, is unconditioned and is the birth right of all, regardless of semantic difference.

The veil of obscuration that has covered over that innate purity of original blessing has been thoroughly cut asunder by the sharp blade of Manjushri, dividing cleanly division itself. This final cutting through of the cardiac ligature is what Advaita calls *krta krtyata*, one that has done all that is to be done. One who can join in on the chorus of:

"It is finished."

Another word for finished is complete, full, perfect. The Great Perfection takes us back to the home which we never left by teaching us until we forget everything else except for our original and blessed purity from the absolute beginning. Christ calls us to lack nothing, just as he lacks nothing. To lack nothing is not to be an isolated and self-contained entity, but to include *everything*. To be all-pervading like space, enveloping and threading through the entire phenomenal universe. To be who we truly are is in essence to be *infinite*.

> "Om, the knower of the Godhead is of one undivided nature with the Supreme. That is Truth, Knowledge, Infinite. One who comes to rest in this, desires nothing, having every desire fulfilled upon arising."

> Taittiriya Upanishad 2.1.1*

This universe appears not just *to* us, not just *in* us, but *as* us. The entire drama is the glamour of our own innate capacity of reflection. Because both the unborn face, and its mysterious reflection are non-dual as the glimmering of being-knowing, the whole is without any seams or demarcations and truly edgeless.

This infinity is referred to by the Vedantic mediated definition of Brahman as ānanda, bliss. Though to prevent us from mistaking it for some extraordinary experience, Abhinavagupta in his *Anuttarastika* says, "This bliss is not like the intoxication of wine or that of riches, nor similar to the union with the beloved. The light of manifestation is not like the ray of light from a lamp, sun, or moon. When one frees oneself from accumulated multiplicity, the state of bliss is like that of putting down a burden."

But what does that perfection look like from the outside? How does the person of wisdom live in the world after coming to see how things really are? Jesus encourages us with the beatitudes in his trademark way by saying:

> "In this way you may become sons of your Father in the heavens, for he makes his sun to rise on the wicked and the good, and sends rain upon the just and the unjust. For if you love only those who love you, what recompense do you have? Do not even the tax-collectors do the same? And if you greet only your brothers, what are you doing that is extraordinary? Do not even the gentiles do the same? So be perfect, as your Heavenly Father is perfect."

Because when we see our own innate purity, the natural outflow of that wisdom is unshakeable *compassion*. The true heart of Christ is always with those in abject poverty of spirit. And what this radical kenosis does, is not divorce us from the relative realm of phenomenon to the separate noumenon—rather, it reveals the unreality of their separation in the least.

Those that are truly alone *(monakhos)*, know that they are with the whole world, and that every face is Christ in disguise. That *all* this is verily Brahman, and that if there's ever wisdom divorced from compassion...

It's not wisdom *at all.*

To unite wisdom and compassion is to truly be *amrta,* deathless. When the body goes, you will remain. But it is also a birthlessness. Ones recognition of I becomes homogenous throughout the three times of past, present, and future. This birthless and deathless nature *is* The Life Eternal that Christ so deep-heartedly told us about. The Vedanta calls it *jivanmukti,* free in this very life.

This freedom expresses naturally as song from a bird, as sweetness from honey, as softness from fleece, as light from a flame.

Words can never contain the truth, but *neither can silence.*

Because although, yes, silence is God's first language. Her second is *poetry.*

In an effort to retain the highest fidelity in our theory and practice, we can seclude ourselves in forests, in retreat centers, in speech, and in thought. Hearing the refrain echoed for novices that real truth isn't contained in words, but in silence.

However, God Herself is a paradox of emptiness and fullness that *even silence cannot contain.*

The Taittiriya Upanishad bellows,

"..that from which speech and the mind turn back, not having reached it." (2.9.1)

And yet later, that it rests in speech, in rain that nourishes the field, in the light of the stars.

As St Teresa of Avila said, "To give our Lord a perfect hospitality, Mary and Martha must combine."[29] And in their sublation, their non-duality echoes what Ruysbroeck terms the "two-fold property of the Godhead": repose, and fecundity.

The irony rushes in as all our effort to clumsily divide the Self into static and dynamic poles collapses. We're inundated not with austere reverence, but with the bright dalliance of *laughter.*

Of course, words can never contain the mystery. But I tell you:

Even the silence is deafening compared to the quietude of God's movement.

God is bilingual. And not just in separately demarcated times depending on who's listening. She weaves in and out of the spoken and the unspoken like a lifelong polyglot, dreaming in the lexicon of both stillness and of motion. Far from being imprisoned in the jail of our contemplative silence, the Divine is utterly *free* in its display. Not as the lofty and unknowable Godhead, but *infinitely* knowable as the boundless light of awareness, without end.

Linguistic mysticism, whether in the Semitic, or Tantric traditions confirms: the spoken or written word does not diminish the Real by one quarter spoonful. In fact, it is the inherent capacity of the self-revealing nature of the Self to kenotically pour itself into reality as The Word. Despite never being able to encapsulate the fullness of truth in words, to assume that a static quietude encompasses Reality *is also an error.*

And to burst forth like light from a tomb, with the joy of the manifold in expression of what we know is inexpressible is in itself, *holy.*

Despite our unfailing belief in the reality of appearances, we cling to the certainty of our unknowing. Holding out hope that one day, in the great by and by, we might become graced with a flash of clarity. And if we do receive it, we will humbly take our crumb back to the small, dimly lit hole we've chewed out for ourselves in the baseboard of God's infinite abode. But we sell ourselves short.

This precious human birth, this moment of opportunity is what we've been waiting for since time immemorial. We need not settle for a flash in the pan, or a glimpse of true peace amidst the background of suffering. We need not piously worship the doorframe instead of boldly walking through it, feeling that the bridal chamber is for higher souls.

There *is* no soul higher than yours.
You are not the dark room, but the open flame.

So, burn, and in your burning be not illumined, but be illumination itself. Because it is not enough to be merely illumined.

You must become all light.

Really, you already are. And that's the good news.

"In pure presence, which is free of dualistic perception, the intrinsic radiance of present awareness shines out. Like a rainbow appearing vividly in the sky, the light of awareness glows in the matrix of reality. That light is all pervading without center or circumference."

Keith Dowman, *Everything is Light*
Thig le Kun gsal chen po 'i rgyud
The Circle of Total Illumination

Afterword

- Krishnamurti

POST-ENLIGHTENMENT SADHANA

My teachers most frequently invoked verse of scripture is forever worn into the grooves of my memory.

Vivekachudamani, shloka 267 *thunders:*

> "Even after the realization of Truth, there remains a powerful, beginningless, deep impression that one is the doer and the enjoyer, which is the cause for rebirth. It has to be conscientiously rooted out by living in unceasing identification with the Self. The annihilation of the vāsanās, here and now, is called Liberation by the wise."

We never *fully* arrive. At least not as a person. Because ultimately, we never left. But that's not an excuse to get caught in a loop where we justify our own suffering. Sacred texts might say that a certain person achieved enlightenment on this day, or was liberated at this time. But this really isn't the end of the journey, but the beginning and we must hasten slowly. After the recognition of our true nature, the unfolding of that realization like a rose in the body and mind by the affection of grace is an *ongoing process*. It's said that the journey to God has an end, but the journey *in* God is *endless*.

All of reality is simply zero blooming into infinity. Really, they're the same, but seem conceptually superimposed in the hypostasis of Being and Becoming. Becoming is already Being, and Being forever appears as Becoming. As vagabonds of that eternal bloom there will naturally be a collection of moments where our old habits spin along like a dusty ceiling fan after you flick the off-switch. Stability is not something to be attained, but rather something to be revealed. We attain stability not by adding on, but by removing the unstable. That stabilization of the resonance between the view, meditation, and result prevents us from taking flashes of realization as the end of the path, and being appropriated by the ego. As such, the teaching on stability is helpful to keep us from being 'phony holy'.

But like all things in this world, even our best intentions can be taken captive by the appropriative faculty of the mind. We might become lost in the dense forest of sacred texts, captive to retreat after retreat, and seminar after seminar. We may tag along to teacher after teacher, afraid to step into our own fullness. Playing the fool, we can chase past spiritual experiences thinking that we had it at one point, but then lost it somehow. We can become stuck in a never-ending loop of striving to stabilize the recognition by effort through meditative techniques and practices to open subtle channels. By the forcing of the mind into artificial and fabricated states of silence and stillness, by a death grip on conceptual elaboration. We may even perhaps become spiritually jaded enough to believe that it's all about the journey of perpetual seeking, and that despite what the masters have said, that there may not be such a thing as freedom in this life.

Despite what Saint Paul said, the mind of Christ *cannot be put on*, as if it was other than the root of our innermost being. Instead, it is unveiled to itself, from itself, by itself.[30] Like the house built on solid rock in Jesus' teaching, we reach the changeless by removing the unstable sands of change. Just as a vast mountain retains its stillness as the sea of fog envelops it, we attain to stability when we recognize ourself as untouched by the ephemeral. We fulfill our inherent potential when we rest in the nature of transience as the bliss of our own innate purity.

There will of course be a period of maturation, a deepening of realization, absorbing the tannins from the oak of our body. Eventually that wineskin will not be able to contain the old wine and will spill out. But the wine is never ruined, it simply spills continuously into ever new, ever greater wineskins.

It's wineskins, or more accurately, wine—all the way down.

The Self has been called a continuum of mysterious creativity, because it is completely fulfilled in knowing itself infinitely. The Chandogya Upanishad speaks of it as poreless solidity of bliss-consciousness. And that bliss revels in its own perfection through the lightshow of space and time. So for now, in your practice, notice the ways that you're looking for 'completion' or finality. Be aware of any acute sense of wanting to finish or conclude your path by receiving the highest transmission or jhana, reading the rarest text, taking the most intensive course.

And if anyone ever tells you they've reached the end, ask them:

What end?

Acknowledgments

This book would not have been possible without the precious support of every person I've ever met. Every soul has led me gently along the way, or oftentimes dragged me with ruthless honesty. Of those that I can name, I would like to include my father and mother, for loving me as imperfectly perfect as they knew how. My spiritual teachers, Lama Michael, Acarya Staneshwar Timalsina, Sri Ram, and Father Richard Rohr. My guru Jim Gilman, for repeatedly holding up the mirror and showing me the true nature of mind. My wife, for showing me what it means to truly be kind. And to my two dogs, Luna and Stella, who give me the opportunity to practice joy for no reason at all.

Glossary

A

Adam: In the context of Christian theology, Adam is often regarded as the first man created by God and represents humanity's initial disobedience and fall from grace. For our purposes, he symbolizes the universal human condition and identity in Christian theology, often regarded as the first man created by God.

Advaita: A Sanskrit term meaning "not two"; A school of Hindu philosophy emphasizing non-dualism, asserting the essential unity of the soul (Atman) and the ultimate reality (Brahman), positing that the apparent multiplicity of the universe is just how things look, not how things are.

Adhyaropa (Adhyasa): The process of superimposition where attributes of one thing are mistakenly attributed to another, such as seeing the self in the not-self (e.g., the body, mind). In Vedanta, it refers to the projection of ignorance that leads to a misperception of the self and the universe.

Anatman: In Buddhism, the doctrine of "not-self" that denies the existence of a permanent, unchanging soul or self. It encourages the realization of emptiness and the interconnectedness of all things.

Adhikari: In spiritual context, a person deemed competent or qualified for receiving a particular teaching or undertaking a specific spiritual practice.

Ahamkara: The ego or "I-maker," the aspect of the mind that identifies with the individual self and differentiates it from the rest of existence. The sense of individuality that arises from identifying with one's body and mind, obscuring the realization of the true self (Atman) as non-dual and unified with Brahman.

Ajata Vada: A doctrine of Advaita Vedanta which posits that the world has never been created, challenging the notion of origination, and emphasizing the non-dual nature of reality.

Anubhava Vākya: Expressions reflecting direct experiential realization of the ultimate truth, emphasizing the non-dual nature of consciousness.

Anusandhāna Vākya: The conclusive realization affirming the non-separation of self and Brahman, emphasizing the unity of all existence, and serving as the culmination of spiritual inquiry in Vedanta.

Aparokshanubhuti: A Sanskrit term meaning direct or immediate experience of the ultimate reality, as opposed to indirect or conceptual knowledge.

Apatheia (Dispassion): A state of inner peace and equanimity, free from passionate desires and aversions. It's a goal in both

Stoic philosophy and early Christian monasticism, indicating a purified heart responsive to God's will.

Apophatic Theology (Via Negativa): A theological approach that emphasizes knowing God by negation, recognizing that God's essence transcends human understanding and language. Asceticism (Askêsis): Spiritual practices of self-denial or discipline aimed at achieving a deeper spiritual state or understanding.

Atman: The true self or soul in Hindu philosophy, regarded as eternal, unchanging, and identical across all beings, emphasizing the non-dualistic essence beyond physical and mental constructs.

Avidya: A Sanskrit term from Indian philosophy meaning ignorance or misconception, particularly the misunderstanding of the nature of the self and the reality, which leads to suffering and bondage in the cycle of rebirths (samsara).

Avyopadeśa: Describes the indescribable nature of the Self, emphasizing that the true essence of being transcends language and conceptual understanding.

B

Beatitude: Supreme blessedness, auspiciousness.

Bhagavad Gita: A 700-verse Hindu scripture that is part of the Indian epic Mahabharata. It consists of a conversation between Prince Arjuna and the god Krishna, who serves as his charioteer.

Bhakti: The path of devotion and love towards God. In Hinduism, bhakti yoga is a spiritual practice centered around loving devotion towards a personal deity, leading to union with the divine.

Brahman: The ultimate, formless reality in Hinduism, beyond individual existence, serving as the source of all material and spiritual life, characterized by its limitless, unchanging nature.

Brahmanishta: Individuals firmly rooted in the realization of Brahman, embodying spiritual wisdom and living in continuous awareness of the non-dual reality.

C

Catushpada: Refers to the four parts or quarters of Atman as described in the Mandukya Upanishad, symbolizing different states of consciousness but ultimately pointing to their unity in the singular reality of Brahman.

Contemplation: A deep, reflective, and loving attention to the divine reality, beyond mere intellectual understanding, leading to an intimate encounter with the divine presence.

D

Da'ath: A Hebrew word for knowledge that encompasses intimacy and direct experience. It's used in the Bible to describe profound, experiential knowledge, including the intimate union between individuals.

Dark Night of the Sense and Soul: Terms used by St. John of the Cross to describe periods of spiritual dryness and existential crisis that lead to deeper purification and eventual closeness to God.

Divine Union (Deification): The process of becoming fully united with God, resulting in a transformation that aligns one's will and nature with the divine leading to a profound sense of oneness with God.

Dvaita: A school of Vedanta philosophy that interprets the Upanishads as teaching a strict dualism between God (the Supreme Being) and individual souls. "Dvaita" translates to "two" in Sanskrit, indicating the irreducible difference between God and the human soul.

Dzogchen: A tradition of teachings in Tibetan Buddhism aimed at discovering the natural primordial state.

E

Economic Trinity vs. Immanent Trinity: Differentiates God's activities in the world (Economic) from the internal relations within God's own being (Immanent).

Epistemology: The study of knowledge, its nature, and limits.

F

Forgiveness: Letting go of grievances, recognizing the innocence of others. And further, that there are no others.

G

Gnosis: Knowledge of spiritual truths, often mystical or esoteric in nature.

H

Hermeneutics: The study of interpretation theory; in religious contexts, it refers to the methodology applied in interpreting religious texts, such as the Bible or the Upanishads.

Hero's Journey: A common template of stories involving a transformative adventure.

I

Iconoclasm: The destruction of religious idols.

Illumination: A stage in spiritual development marked by an influx of divine qualities such as peace, compassion, and insight.

J

Jñana (Gnosis): Spiritual knowledge or enlightenment, especially the direct experiential knowledge of the divine or ultimate reality. In Hinduism, jñana yoga is the path of knowledge, aiming for realization through the understanding of the self's oneness with Brahman.

Jñanis: Individuals who have attained profound spiritual wisdom through self-realization.

Jiva: In Indian philosophy, it refers to the individual soul or living being, characterized by its consciousness and karma. It is often contrasted with Brahman, the ultimate reality or universal soul.

Jivanmukti: Liberation while alive, characterized by the realization of one's unity with Brahman, leading to freedom from the cycle of rebirth and dissolution of ego.

K

Kaivalya: In Indian philosophy, especially in Yoga and Advaita Vedanta, it refers to the ultimate state of self-determination or liberation, where the soul is free from the bondage of the material and mental worlds.

Karma Yoga: The path in Hinduism focusing on selfless service and action in the world as a form of worship and a way to spiritual liberation, without attachment to the outcomes.

Kenosis: A Greek term used in Christian theology to describe the self-emptying of Jesus' own will and becoming entirely receptive to God's divine will. It is a model for spiritual humility and the path towards Divine Union by dissolution of ego and individual distinctions to realize unity with the divine.

Krta Krtyata: The state of having accomplished all that is to be done, indicating spiritual completion where the individual experiences unity with Brahman and transcends worldly desires.

L

Lectio Divina: Traditional monastic practice in Western Christianity that involves reading, meditating, and praying on scripture.

Logos: A borrowed term from Stoic philosophy. In Christian theology, refers to Jesus Christ as the divine reason and Word of God, the macrocosmic blueprint of all creation implicit in the cosmos, ordering it and giving it form and meaning.

M

Madhvācārya: Founder of the Dvaita school of Vedanta, emphasizing the dualism between God and souls.

Mahavakyas: Principal statements from the Upanishads encapsulating the essence of Vedantic non-dualism, expressing the unity of Atman and Brahman and the realization of non-duality.

Mandala: A spiritual and ritual symbol representing the aesthetic symmetry of the universe in Hinduism and Buddhism.

Metanoia: A transformative change of heart by going beyond the mind; spiritual conversion or awakening.

Metaphysics: A branch of philosophy that investigates the fundamental nature of reality, including the relationship between mind and matter, substance and attribute, and potentiality and actuality.

Moksha: In Indian religions, it represents liberation from the cycle of death and rebirth (samsara). It is the ultimate spiritual goal in Hinduism.

Mumukshutva: A term borrowed from Hindu philosophy, referring to the intense longing for liberation or release from the cycle of birth and death (samsara). In a Christian context, it denotes a deep desire for spiritual freedom and union with God.

Mythical Allegory: A narrative that has a secondary meaning beneath the surface one, often used in religious texts to convey spiritual truths through symbolic stories.

N

Nescience: Primordial and fundamental ignorance.

Neti-neti: A method of discriminative negation used in Advaita Vedanta to remove adjuncts and isolate the natural essence of the Self.

Non-Action (Wu-Wei): A Taoist concept emphasizing action that is effortless and in harmony with the natural flow of the universe, without forced effort or attachment to results.

Non-Dualism: A philosophical viewpoint based on direct experiential realization that there is no fundamental distinction between the mind and the physical world, or between God and the universe.

Non-Dual Awareness: Transcendence of the distinction between the triad of subject, means of knowledge, and object. Nirvana: In Buddhism, the ultimate state free from suffering and the cycle of rebirth. It represents the extinguishing of the fires of desire, aversion, and ignorance.

Nirvikalpa: The trans-rational state of mind when all thought has been stilled, and the clarity of awareness is like a steady flame in a windless place.

O

Original Blessing: A concept introduced by Matthew Fox, contrasting with the doctrine of original sin. It emphasizes humanity's inherent goodness, created in the image of God (Imago Dei), and the world's fundamental positivity.

Original Sin: A Christian doctrine stating that humanity inherits a fallen nature due to Adam's disobedience. This condition is characterized by an inherent tendency towards sin, necessitating divine grace for salvation.

P

Pancadasi: A robust instructional text by Śri Vidyaranya in the Advaita Vedanta tradition.

Panentheism: The belief that God pervades the universe but is also beyond it.

Pancakoshas: The five sheaths or coverings that, according to Vedanta, obscure the true Self (Atman) within the human being: the physical body, the energy body, the mental body, the wisdom body, and the bliss body.

Panentheism: The belief that God pervades the universe but is also beyond it; unlike pantheism, which posits that God is synonymous with the universe, panentheism maintains a distinction but insists that the universe is contained within God.

Parokśa Jñana: Indirect or conceptual knowledge about reality, as opposed to direct or experiential knowledge (Aparokśa Jñana).

Perichoresis: Describes the interpenetration and co-inherence of the Trinity in Christian theology, suggesting a model for understanding the relational aspect of divine unity.

Pramana: In Indian philosophy, pramana is the means by which one obtains accurate and valid knowledge.

Prayer of Recollection: A form of prayer that involves gathering one's faculties together to focus entirely on the presence of God. It is a stepping stone toward deeper forms of meditation and contemplative prayer.

Procession and Return: A neo-Platonic theme found in spiritual traditions, describing the emanation of all things from the One (procession) and their eventual return or reintegration back into the One.

Purgation: The initial phase of the contemplative journey, where individuals seek to detach from worldly desires and distractions to focus more deeply on spiritual growth and connection with God.

Q

Qualified Non-Dualism: A viewpoint within Vedantic philosophy, particularly associated with Ramanuja, that posits a fundamental oneness in existence, with God as the underlying reality. However, it also acknowledges the reality of diversity within the universe, making it a "qualified" form of non-dualism.

R

Raja Yoga: The "royal path" of yoga, emphasizing meditation and mental control.

Ramanuja: Proponent of the Vishistadvaita school of Vedanta, advocating a qualified non-dualism.

S

Salvation: In Christianity, the deliverance from sin and its consequences, believed by Christians to be brought about by faith in Christ.

Śakta Tantra: A branch of Hinduism focusing on the worship of the goddess Shakti as the Absolute.

Sakshin: The witness consciousness; in Vedanta, the pure, unattached awareness that observes all mental and physical phenomena without identifying with them.

Samādiṣaṭkasampatti: A set of six virtues in Vedanta that are essential for spiritual growth: tranquility, control, withdrawal, forbearance, faith, and concentration.

Samsara: The cycle of death and rebirth to which life in the material world is bound.

Sankalpa: A willful desire or intention. When limited, acts as an obscuration to insight, but when unlimited, as a means for the fullness of insight.

Satchitananda: Describes the nature of reality as the ground of being, infinite consciousness, and bliss absolute.

Sattvic: Derived from Sattva, one of the three Gunas (qualities) in Hindu and yogic philosophy, indicating purity, harmony, and balance, often associated with a state conducive to spiritual growth and enlightenment.

Self-Inquiry (Atma Vichara): A method of spiritual practice recommended by Śri Ramana Maharshi, focusing on the introspective question "Who am I?" to dissolve the ego and reveal the true Self.

Semantic: Relating to meaning in language or logic.

Semitic and Greek culture: Cultural and linguistic influences from Jewish peoples and ancient Greeks.

Solipsism: the errant philosophical theory that the individual ego is all that exists.

Spiritual Ego: The ego that can arise within spiritual contexts, characterized by pride in one's spiritual achievements or a sense of superiority over those perceived as less spiritually advanced.

Spiritual Oscillation: Fluctuating between spiritual highs and lows as part of the spiritual journey.

Srotriya, Brahmanishta, Karuna: Qualities of a true spiritual teacher in Vedanta. Respectively, being learned in scriptures, established in the realization of the ultimate reality (Brahman), and embodying infinite compassion.

Synoptic Gospels: The Gospels of Matthew, Mark, and Luke, sharing many of the same stories.

T

Tapasya: A Sanskrit term for heat, especially the heat generated by spiritual practice, austerity, or severe discipline. It symbolizes the purifying energy that burns away impurities.

Theosis: The process of becoming divine or partaking in the divine nature in Christian mysticism, especially within Eastern Orthodox tradition, seen as the goal of spiritual life.

Theophany: A visible manifestation to humankind of God or a god.

Trinity: In Christian doctrine, the unity of Father, Son, and Holy Spirit as three persons in one Godhead.

U

Upanishads: A collection of ancient Sanskrit texts that contain some of the central philosophical concepts and ideas of Hinduism, among them, the concept of Brahman (the ultimate reality) and Atman (the individual soul), forming the core of Indian philosophical thought.

Upadeśa Vākya: Spiritual instruction or teaching statement that provides direct guidance towards realizing one's true nature.

V

Vairagya (Detachment): The quality of dispassion or detachment from desires and possessions, considered essential for spiritual growth and realization of the self's unity with the divine.

Vedanta: Literally the end or finality of the Vedas. One of the six orthodox schools of Hindu philosophy, based on the teachings of the Upanishads. It focuses on meditation, morality, and spiritual knowledge, with various interpretations such as Advaita (non-dualism), Dvaita (dualism), and Vishistadvaita (qualified non-dualism).

Via Negativa (Apophatic Theology): Describing God by specifying what God is not.

Vivekachudamani (Crest Jewel of Discrimination): A Sanskrit text attributed to Adi Shankara that expounds on the philosophy of non-dualism (Advaita Vedanta) and describes the traits of a qualified teacher and a spiritually prepared student.

Vyapti: A principle of mutual concomitance or pervasiveness, where the presence of one thing invariably indicates the presence of another, used in Vedanta to illustrate the inseparability of the observer and the observed, or consciousness and its manifestations.

Bibliography

Adyashanti. Resurrecting Jesus : Embodying the Spirit of a
        Revolutionary Mystic. Sounds True, 2016.

Al-'Arabi Ibn. Whoso Knoweth Himself. Beshara, 1977.

Aṣṭāvakra, and Swami Nityaswarupananda. Aṣṭāvakra Gītā =
        Aṣṭāvakra Gītā = Ashtavakra Gita. Sri Ramanasramam,
        2011.

Barnhart, Bruno. The Golden String BULLETIN of the BEDE
        GRIFFITHS TRUST NONDUALITY in the VEDIC
        and BIBLICAL TRADITIONS John Martin
        AUGUSTINE and the WISDOM of the WEST. 2002,
        www.bedegriffiths.com/wp-
        content/uploads/2016/05/V9N1.pdf. Accessed 31 Jan.
        2024.

Bisbe, Isaac, and Holy Transfiguration Monastery (Boston,
        Massachusetts. The Ascetical Homilies of Saint Isaac the
        Syrian. The Holy Transfiguration Monastery, 2011.

Bourgeault, Cynthia. The Holy Trinity and the Law of Three :
        Discovering the Radical Truth at the Heart of
        Christianity. Shambhala, 2013.

Calvin, Jean, et al. Calvin : Institutes of the Christian Religion.
        Westminster John Knox Press, 2011.

David Bentley Hart. The Experience of God. Yale University
Press, 2013.

---. The New Testament. Yale University Press, 2023.

---. You Are Gods : On Nature and Supernature. University Of
Notre Dame Press, 2022.

David Peter Lawrence. The Teachings of the Odd-Eyed One.
State University of New York Press, 2008.

De la Cruz, Juan. The Living Flame of Love by St. John of the
Cross with His Letters, Poems, and Minor Writings.
Cosimo, Inc., 2007.

de, Nicolás. Nicolai de Cusa Opera Omnia. Translated by
Bernard Mcginn, vol. VI: 17-19, Felix Meiner Verlag,
Hamburg., 1970, pp. 44–46.

Dowman, Keith. Everything Is Light : The Great Explanatory
Dzogchen Tantra Thig Le Kun Gsal Chen Po'i Rgyud :
The Circle of Total Illumination. Dzogchen Now!
Books, 2017.

Easwaran Eknath. The Bhagavad Gita. Nilgiri Press, 2019.

Fowler, Jeaneane D. Perspectives of Reality. Liverpool
University Press, 2002.

Grant, Sara. Toward an Alternative Theology. 2002.

Griffiths, Bede. The New Creation in Christ. Templegate Pub,
1994.

Hadley, Judith M. The Cult of Asherah in Ancient Israel and
　　　　Judah : Evidence for a Hebrew Goddess. Cambridge
　　　　University Press, 2000.

Ilia Delio. The Unbearable Wholeness of Being : God, Evolution
　　　　and the Power of Love. Orbis Books, 2014, p. 79.

Jan van Ruusbroec. Werken van Jan van Ruusbroec. Mechelen:
　　　　Het Kompas, 1932-1934, 1858, p. 246.

Jan Van Ruysbroeck. The Adornment of the Spiritual Marriage.
　　　　Cosimo, Inc., 2007.

Jean-Yves Leloup, and Joseph Rowe. The Gospel of Thomas :
　　　　The Gnostic Wisdom of Jesus. Inner Traditions, 2005.

Julian, Of Norwich, et al. Revelations of Divine Love : Short
　　　　Text and Long Text. Penguin Books, 1998, p. 144.

Mcginn, Bernard. The Essential Writings of Christian Mysticism.
　　　　Modern Library, 2006.

of the Cross, John. The Ascent of Mount Carmel. 1922.

Of, Teresa, and Mirabai Starr. The Interior Castle. Riverhead
　　　　Books, 2003.

Palamas, Gregory, et al. The One Hundred and Fifty Chapters.
　　　　Pontifical Institute Of Mediaeval Studies, 1988.

Porete, Marguerite, et al. The Mirror of Simple Souls. University
　　　　Of Notre Dame Press, 1999.

Prabhavananda, Swami, and Ramakrishna Math. Srimad
　　　　Bhagavatam. Sri Ramakrishna Math, 2011.

Progoff, Ira. The Cloud of Unknowing. Introductory
        Commentary and Translation by Ira Progoff. Random
        House Publishing, 1959.

Raimon Panikkar, and Raimundo Panikkar. Christophany. Faith
        Meets Faith, 2004, pp. 72–73.

Saint, Augustine,. Augustine. 1: Introduction and Text :
        Confessions. Oxford University Press, 2012.

Śaṅkarācārya, et al. Dṛg Dṛśya Viveka. Central Chinmaya Mission
        Trust, 2010.

Śaṅkarācārya. Brahma-Sūtra-Bhāsya of Śrī Śaṅkarācārya.
        Ramakrishna Math, 1965.

Soren Kierkegaard. Purity of Heart. Harper Collins, 2011.

Swami Chetanananda. Avadhuta Gita of Dattatreya. Advaita
        Ashrama (A Publication House of Ramakrishna Math,
        Belur Math), 1984.

Swami Chinmayananda. Aitareya Upanishad. Central Chinmaya
        Mission Trust, 2017, pp. 135–36.

---. Ashtavakra Gita - Song of Self Realization. Central Chinmaya
        Mission Trust, 2018.

---. Atmabodha. Central Chinmaya Mission Trust, 2013.

---. Isavasya Upanishad. Central Chinmaya Mission Trust, 2015.

---. Kathopanisad. Central Chinmaya Mission Trust, 2013.

---. Kenopanisad. Central Chinmaya Mission Trust, 2013.

---. Mandukya Upanishad with Gaudapada's Karika. Central Chinmaya Mission Trust, 2017.

---. Mundakopanisad. Central Chinmaya Mission Trust, 2013.

---. Shankara's Vivekacudamani. Central Chinmaya Mission Trust, 1991.

---. Taittiriya Upanishad. Central Chinmaya Mission Trust, 2014.

---. The Holy Geeta. Mumbai Central Chinmaya Mission Trust, 2013.

Swami Gambhirananda. Mundaka Upanishad with Commentary of Shankara. Ramakrishna Math, 1978.

Swami Jagadananda. Upadesa Sahasri. Sri Ramakrishna Math, 2023.

Swami Ramananda Saraswati. Tripura Rahasya. World Wisdom, Inc, 2002.

Swami Swahananda. Chandogya and Brihadaranyaka Upanishads. Createspace Independent Publishing Platform, 2016.

Swami Vimuktananda. Aparokshanubhuti. Vedanta Press, 1938.

Thomas, Aquinas Saint, and Dominicans. English Province. Summa Theologica. Cosimo Classics, 2007.

Underhill, Evelyn. Mysticism : A Study in Nature and Development of Spiritual Consciousness. Alicia Editions, 2020.

Wallis, Christopher. Recognition Sutras. Mattamayura Press, 2017, p. 73.

Zondervan. NRSVue, Holy Bible. Zondervan, 2022.

About the Author

Jory Pryor resides on the Eastern Shore of Maryland with his wife Michelle, and two boston terriers, Luna and Stella. He offers virtual and asynchronous spiritual direction to dedicated practitioners of all backgrounds.

www.methodsofcontemplation.com

End Notes

---

[1] ---. *You Are Gods : On Nature and Supernature.* University Of Notre Dame Press, 2022, pp. 121.

[2] Swami Jagadananda. *Upadesa Sahasri.* Sri Ramakrishna Math, 2023.

[3] Saint, Augustine,. Augustine. 1: Introduction and Text : Confessions. Oxford University Press, 2012.

[4] of the Cross, John. *The Ascent of Mount Carmel.* 1922.

[5] Soren Kierkegaard. Purity of Heart. Harper Collins, 2011.

[6] Raimon Panikkar, and Raimundo Panikkar. *Christophany.* Faith Meets Faith, 2004, pp. xv.

[7] Progoff, Ira. *The Cloud of Unknowing. Introductory Commentary and Translation by Ira Progoff.* 1959.

[8] of the Cross, John. *The Ascent of Mount Carmel.* 1922.

[9] Bourgeault, Cynthia. *The Holy Trinity and the Law of Three : Discovering the Radical Truth at the Heart of Christianity.* Shambhala, 2013.

[10] Julian, Of Norwich, et al. *Revelations of Divine Love : Short Text and Long Text.* Penguin Books, 1998, p. 144.

[11] Underhill, Evelyn. *Mysticism : A Study in Nature and Development of Spiritual Consciousness.* Alicia Editions, 2020.

[12] Grant, Sara. Toward an Alternative Theology. 2002.

[13] Griffiths, Bede. *The New Creation in Christ*. Templegate Pub, 1994.

[14] Hadley, Judith M. *The Cult of Asherah in Ancient Israel and Judah :Evidence for a Hebrew Goddess*. Cambridge University Press, 2000.

[15] Thomas, Aquinas Saint, and Dominicans. English Province. *Summa Theologica*. Cosimo Classics, 2007.

[16] David Bentley Hart. *The New Testament*. Yale University Press, 2023.

[17] de, Nicolás. Nicolai de Cusa Opera Omnia. Translated by Bernard Mcginn, vol. VI: 17-19, Felix Meiner Verlag, Hamburg., 1970, pp. 44–46.

[18] Mcginn, Bernard. *The Essential Writings of Christian Mysticism*. Modern Library, 2006.

[19] Palamas, Gregory, et al. *The One Hundred and Fifty Chapters*. Pontifical Institute Of Mediaeval Studies, 1988.

[20] Mcginn, Bernard. *The Essential Writings of Christian Mysticism*. Modern Library, 2006.

[21] Saint, Augustine,. *Augustine. 1: Introduction and Text : Confessions*. Oxford University Press, 2012.

[22] Jan Van Ruysbroeck. *The Adornment of the Spiritual Marriage*. Cosimo, Inc., 2007.

[23] Underhill, Evelyn. *Mysticism : A Study in Nature and Development*

of *Spiritual Consciousness*. Alicia Editions, 2020.

24 Jan Van Ruysbroeck. *The Adornment of the Spiritual Marriage.*
Cosimo, Inc., 2007.

25 Adyashanti. *Resurrecting Jesus : Embodying the Spirit of a
Revolutionary Mystic.* Sounds True, 2016.

26 Wallis, Christopher. Recognition Sutras. Mattamayura Press,
2017, p. 73.

27 Raimon Panikkar, and Raimundo Panikkar. *Christophany.* Faith
Meets Faith, 2004, pp. 72–73.

28 ---. *You Are Gods : On Nature and Supernature.* University Of
Notre Dame Press, 2022.

29 Of, Teresa, and Mirabai Starr. *The Interior Castle.* Riverhead
Books, 2003.

30 Al-'Arabi Ibn. Whoso Knoweth Himself. Beshara, 1977.